The
Mid-Life
Makeover
Method

Inspired Life Publishing
A division of The Inspiration Center, LLC
11821 – 246TH STREET
LAWRENCE, KANSAS 66044

ISBN: 979-8-9860061-1-6   ebook
         979-8-9860061-0-9   paperback

Library of Congress Control Number: 2022906010

First Edition
Book Production by Brands Through Books
brandsthroughbooks.com

Author photography by Johanna Dye Photography
johannadye.com
Inspired Life Publishing logo by Darleen Schillaci

cindydwhitmer.com

The Mid-Life Makeover Method

The Secret to Loving Yourself Fully and Living on Your Terms

CINDY D. WHITMER

Inspired Life Publishing

A division of The Inspiration Center, LLC

"This compelling book takes us on a journey through the trials and tribulations of mid-life for the author and many other women who all learned how to change the trajectory of their lives using *The Mid-Life Makeover Method*. Ms. Whitmer offers the way out of the struggles of mid-life into one that is joy-filled, meaningful, and leaves the reader looking forward to the future instead of dreading it."

—JACK CANFIELD, Coauthor of the *Chicken Soup for the Soul*® series and *The Success Principles*™: *How to Get from Where You Are to Where You Want to Be*

"You can buy new shoes, get a face lift, move to a different country. But none of those 'makeovers' will do for you what this book can. A true makeover, one that literally sends your life spinning in new, exciting directions, requires the inner work Cindy writes about in *The Mid-Life Makeover Method*.

"Did I say work? The shifts certainly require unfamiliar excavating, but 'work' doesn't aptly describe the adventure on which Cindy is inviting you. This journey is rewarding, meaningful and, if taken seriously, the best thing that will ever happen to you.

"Consider this book your official invitation. Cindy provides the map, the toolkit, and the inspiration.

"The six principles in *The Mid-Life Makeover Method* are not some pie-in-the-sky, cross-your-fingers theory. My dear friend Cindy is living proof that they work."

—PAM GROUT, #1 New York Times bestselling author of *E-Squared,
Thank & Grow Rich, Course in Miracles Experiment,*
and seventeen other books

"I love how Cindy helps us celebrate mid-life and all of the magic and possibility it brings. Her *Mid-Life Makeover Method* is what we need in our lives!"

—SUSIE MOORE, bestselling author of *Let It Be Easy*

"Coaching with Cindy is the best investment I have ever made in myself. Her professionalism, knowledge, compassion, and personality are phenomenal. I couldn't get out of my own way, felt alone, overwhelmed, stuck, and very hard on myself. I was in a cycle of self-sabotage. Through coaching with Cindy, I was able to learn to see myself for who I am, become clear on what I want, understand my core beliefs, and set boundaries in all aspects of my life. I am no longer a doormat! All of my relationships have improved significantly. I have the tools to work through anything. I truly feel like there isn't anything I cannot handle."

—DAWN ALBANESE, Connecticut
Member of The 90-Day Mid-Life Makeover Private Coaching Program

"A couple years ago, I started a new journey in life. I was struggling with who I [was], what I [was] about, where I was going, how I was going to get there, and why. I bought self-help books, listened to TED Talks, and had endless conversations with family and friends. Nothing was sticking or making any sense. I continued to feel lost, unworthy, and paralyzed. The experiences with Cindy's coaching program have helped me believe in myself and hold my head high. I learned I can never fail, and I always have a choice. I am living my best life!"

—MELISSA SNOOTS, Ohio
Member of The 90-Day Mid-Life Makeover Private Coaching Program

"I was going through a tough time in my professional life and realized my confidence was at an all-time low. Cindy's experience and training [were] just what I needed. She has skills that help you get to the core of things and the tools needed for life going forward. She is truly the best in helping create a life I am truly grateful for. Barely a week goes by where I don't hear her words guiding me through a situation. I am so very grateful to her and for what she continues to contribute to my well-being."

—ANNETTE CLAUSEN, Washington
Member of The Mid-Life Makeover Group

"As my 42-year career in theatre administration was coming to an end, I signed up to take The 90-Day Mid-Life Makeover Private Coaching Program because I realized the magnitude of such a change. Although retiring was incredibly exciting and exactly what I wanted, I realized how much my identity was defined by my career. I wanted to move through this major life change with integrity, grace, and ease. Cindy made that possible. Coaching with her was a very empowering experience, and I am truly grateful."

—KATHERINE PRYOR, Kansas
Member of The Mid-Life Makeover Group

"I have been following Cindy for years, and when I was faced with a major setback, I immediately hired her to help me process what had happened and to focus positive energy on the next chapter of my life. Through The 90-Day Mid-Life Makeover Private Coaching Program, Cindy is helping me find peace with challenges that have hit me in my fifties. I am developing new beliefs and habits that are giving me renewed confidence and strength. Having a coach to support and drive accountability toward the goals I set for myself is a huge thing! I wouldn't be making the same kind of progress without Cindy's compassion and guidance."

—SHERI KWAPISZESKI, North Carolina
Member of The Mid-Life Makeover Group

"I absolutely adore Cindy. She has been more than a coach to me. She has been a mentor, a confidant, my cheerleader, and a gift. Her professionalism has been outstanding. I completely put my trust in her. While we all have issues in life, it is so necessary to find someone who will be in your corner without bias. Thank you, Cindy, for being such a phenomenal support system and helping me to grow stronger and more confident."

—BETH ROSE, Texas
Member of The Mid-Life Makeover Group

"I first met Cindy in 2004 when I sought her expertise in life coaching for my teenage daughter. Having recently retired, I was questioning where to go from here. I was also troubled by some past family issues and current boundary issues with my adult children. Through our coaching sessions, Cindy listened and helped me find ways to resolve my inner conflicts. I cannot express in words what these sessions meant to getting me back on track to enjoying life."

—TAMARA S., Iowa
Member of The 90-Day Mid-Life Makeover Private Coaching Program

"I am so glad I said 'yes' to Cindy's private coaching program. I was going in circles at home and at the office, not getting ahead at all. Today, I am no longer in that same never-ending circle. We made some real progress, but I knew I wasn't done. I realized what all was possible if I kept moving forward, so I signed up for her graduate coaching program which is helping me complete all of my goals."

—PATSY A. PORTER, Kansas
Member of The 90-Day Mid-Life Makeover Private Coaching Program

Table of Contents

For women everywhere
who are still longing for more.

"I wished to live deliberately, to front only the essential facts of life, and see if I could not learn what it had to teach, and not, when I came to die, discover that I had not lived. I did not wish to live what was not life, living is so dear; nor did I wish to practice resignation, unless it was quite necessary. I wanted to live deep."

—HENRY DAVID THOREAU

Introduction

ON A DREARY SUNDAY AFTERNOON IN SEPTEMBER, MY HUSBAND AND I SAT IN OUR gray minivan in the McAlister's parking lot having the same broken-record conversation we'd had every month, once a month, for the past year. Avoiding eye contact, we both just stared out the front windshield at nothing. I was announcing to him *again* that unless we actively worked together on some key trouble areas of our marriage, I would divorce him. I was begging and pleading with him, the love of my life for the past twenty-four years, to hear me, to see me, and to agree to work on our marriage.

I reiterated that I would work on it in whatever form he thought best—marriage counseling, a marriage enrichment retreat, meetings with our pastor, or even talking to his parents whom we respected so very much—*anything*! His response, for the twelfth month in a row, was, "Why are you trying to cause us trouble? We have *everything*! You have *nothing* to complain about! All marriages have 10 percent problems, just like us. You need to just get over it."

Total despair swept through me. *He's never going to change. I'm done. I've tried.* Feelings of sadness, resignation, defeat, hopelessness, and anger welled up inside me. What had happened to me? I felt completely disregarded. His experience of our marriage was drastically different from mine. The tug-of-war inside me was coming to a crossroads. The two teams? Team One wanted to stay married, believed in the state of marriage, and meant it when I said "I do" as a lifelong commitment no matter what. Team Two believed the only route to healthy emotional survival was my leaving. Both teams wanted happiness.

In that moment, I realized one of my tragic mistakes in life was expecting others to change to make me happy. Can you relate? The women I work with realize by mid-life that they have been doing this all along. I had done this with family members, friends, and colleagues, and now I had done it with my husband. Wow. Didn't I know better? I'm a therapist and a coach, and I've spent my entire professional life trying to help people heal their life by taking ownership of it. How had this idea gotten lost within my own life? I had spent years asking him to change this or that, asking for us to work on different parts of our relationship, and asking him to reconsider how he showed up in our relationship. I had just kept thinking he would see the light and make an effort to be different so we could have a healthy marriage.

So, there it is, the truth, the reality—what none of us really want to see in mid-life, or at any time, but what we must be willing to see if we are going to be happy. It *is* up to us! We must take full responsibility for our happiness. Waiting around for other people to change or to follow our recipe for the best life is like waiting for the government to solve the world's problems. It's just not a realistic plan. It just doesn't work.

I'm not saying people can't change. Of course I know they can. That's why I love the work I do with others so very much! I'm sure my husband could have changed if he truly felt the need or desire to, but apparently, he didn't. Our views of the state of our marriage were completely different. If I wanted to be a happy person, I had to change. And one of the greatest changes I needed to make was to learn how to truly love myself fully and live on my own terms. And so, I did. In this book, I'll tell you what worked for me, what has worked for other women I've helped ever since, and therefore, what can undoubtedly work for you.

Chapter One

Mission Impossible . . . Not!

MY NAME IS CINDY D. WHITMER, AND I'M THE MID-LIFE MAKEOVER COACH. I'VE been a therapist, a coach, a speaker, and an author my entire professional life. When my life began to completely unravel in my forties, I went through several kinds of transformations and started to realize that, in one form or another, most women in mid-life were as well. Our visions of the perfect marriage, the perfect children, the white picket fence, aging gracefully, and feeling amazingly alive and full of energy and purpose start to come undone—our lives are unrecognizable compared to the vision we held for so long.

In mid-life, many women start to feel their bodies betraying them. *Why can't we get a good night's sleep?* We wonder, *Who is this woman in the mirror?* Women start to question their purpose, wondering, *Who am I now? What am I supposed to be doing?* And their relationships may look totally different than they had hoped. Their children are gone and don't need them in the same way anymore. Their partners seem more like strangers—aliens in the same house. Their parents are turning into children, very needy, and now they're supposed to take care of them too? Women wonder how and when to make themselves a priority—and if it's even allowed! Eventually, I found my way through and beyond several seasons of upheaval that are common in mid-life by giving myself a makeover.

When I say "makeover," I don't mean the typical overhaul of your outer appearance often associated with that word. I'm not talking about new wardrobes, hairstyles, body sculpting, or skin-care regimens.

I'm referring to a makeover *from the inside out*. This involves developing an understanding of who you are and how you've shown up in your own life. It's about connecting with your beliefs, values, thoughts, feelings, and choices. Giving yourself a makeover of this kind involves examining all areas of your life to identify what's working and what's not working for you, realizing what you really want, and then making adjustments so you can be happier than you've ever been.

This type of makeover leads to changes that are tangible on the outside because you will undoubtedly learn new ways of being—maybe you'll adopt some new habits or alter your relationships or your environments in some ways. Thus, it's a makeover from the inside out.

Through navigating my own mid-life makeover, I learned the crucial skills necessary for making these the best years of my life so far. I'm grateful to tell you that I'm happier than I've ever been. I firmly believe anyone can do this with the right support, information, and determination. So, I'm on a mission to change mid-life for women from being labeled a "crisis" of gargantuan proportions to being one of the sweetest, most meaningful, and joy-filled seasons of their lives. This book contains a method for doing just that.

Destination Mid-Life: How We Got Here

Before we get into the method, let's talk about how we all got here. Where is "here," you ask? "Here" is the middle of your life—most likely in your forties, fifties, or maybe even your sixties—when you reach an unsettling time and ask yourself (just as I did), *What happened to me?*

Here's what happened to many women and maybe to you, too. Many women gave their lives to others whom they loved deeply. They attached their worth to their roles and the services they provided in caring for others. They prioritized other people's needs, often neglecting, or even forgetting about their own. They wrapped their existence around their relationships with others, putting everyone else ahead of themselves. And they did all of this without questioning any of it. They gave their whole heart, all their energy, most of their focus, many of their resources—everything they had—in the name of love.

Women tend to get extremely good at doing this and find tremendous satisfaction in this pursuit. And then, one day, they realize things are changing. People no longer need them in the same way anymore. Or they finally run out of steam. They may see that they have not been loving themselves properly, and now they're tired, overwhelmed, sapped of their energy, and lost. They no longer know who they are, what they want, or what their purpose is anymore.

They find themselves wondering, *Is this* all *there is?*

At the same time, their bodies have changed, their emotions are all over the place, and they feel like an alien in their own house. Their confidence is declining rapidly, and they fear the future. Inside their mind, they wonder if all they have left to look forward to is aging, sickness, and death. They may believe it's all downhill from here. This depresses them.

I cannot tell you how many times I've heard some version of that story—whether in my counseling practice; in my coaching groups; at networking meetings; at professional conferences; or among family, friends, and other associates. And, of course, I've lived it myself.

Often, when women reach the middle of their lives, they find themselves perplexed, sometimes personally and sometimes professionally. This becomes a time of intense reflection; they look back at how they've lived for twenty-plus years, the impact they've had, and the exhaustion and exhilaration they simultaneously feel about every aspect of their lives. Then they look ahead and begin to wonder what's next for them. Their fears begin to surface, and their confidence begins to wane. It's as if women know that something is off, that something needs to change, but they're unsure how or where to begin. Grief, confusion, and depression become close companions.

Facing similar questions about my own life, I was determined to change. But first, I had to get brutally honest with myself and find out what I didn't like about myself and my choices.

For example, I was an overinvolved parent to my children. Over the years, I was their Sunday school teacher, the homeroom mom for both their classes, the Girl Scout leader, the school fundraising chair, the club volleyball coach, and their baptismal class teacher. I don't even remember what else! I attended almost every sporting, music, school, and church event of their lives and drove more miles taking them to rehearsals, practices, and other activities than I could even count. I believed this meant I was a good mother and that if I had needs outside of theirs, those needs could wait. Actually, I almost forgot I had needs. My kids were my top priority. Sound familiar?

Then there was the marriage. My husband and I operated like business partners (with him in charge), keeping the details of the household and calendar running smoothly. We were high-functioning parents together, did ministry at our church together, attended to our families together, and kept our professional lives going (especially his). At the same time, we neglected to keep our romance alive and well. We rarely went out on dates or away for a weekend together. We tag-teamed a lot to manage the details of our lives. Somehow, in our emotional dynamics, we ended up on opposing teams *often*. I felt he was trying to control me *all the time* and that he believed his life was much more of a priority than mine. In response to his superiority complex, I developed all kinds of unhealthy ways to react that were destructive to our relationship. I went from being a nag to a beggar to an angry you-know-what to a depressed, worn-out soul. I could hardly stand myself anymore! Can you relate?

My body and I seemed to be at war as well. My weight fluctuated more times than I could count. No matter what kind of exercise I tried, sometimes I would lose weight and sometimes I would not. If I did lose it, I'd soon gain it all back. In mid-life, sleeplessness also became a regular visitor. My hormones kept changing too, and with that came mood swings—not to mention the headaches and hot flashes . . . ugh. Even though I knew no one's value was dependent upon their size or shape, I was secretly very hard on myself about this and wanted to be at peace with everything changing about my body. You too?

When I would go to the counseling center and listen to other women, I heard story after story similar to mine. Women in mid-life were trying to understand what in the world was happening to their bodies with the unexplained pain, weight fluctuation, waning sexual desire, and countless sleepless nights. They were lost in their relationships and no longer understood their roles as wives, partners, mothers, daughters, and friends. Professionally, they were at a crossroads, either no longer finding satisfaction in their careers or lost in the search for a purposeful endeavor due to having more time on their hands than they'd ever had before. They were really depressed.

Almost every woman I spoke with in my coaching practice questioned who she was, what had happened to her, and if life was all downhill from this point on. My compassion ran deep, and I knew I wanted to change the story of women in mid-life everywhere. So, as I transformed my own life, I developed a step-by-step method to help all women do the same. Since then, I have spent years perfecting and teaching this process to women through my writing, speaking, and coaching programs. Let me introduce you to one of these women now.

Meet Barbara

My coaching client Barbara was married, had two sons, and had a management position she loved. Her life was a litany of schedules, activities, and obligations. On top of all that, she prided herself on making home-cooked meals for her family as often as possible and keeping an orderly home. She was also actively involved in her parents' lives, often making decisions regarding their well-being. Barbara stayed busy at all times, seven days a week, nonstop.

Once she reached her middle years, her sons graduated from high school and moved on to college. Her parents both died. Her job was no longer satisfying, so she resigned. Her husband had always been a big career person too, and that continued to be true.

Suddenly, it seemed, Barbara's life turned quiet. The boys were grown and gone, no longer requiring her constant attention. Her parents were deceased, so all she had left of them were her memories. And because she changed course due to her professional dissatisfaction, the part of her that managed people came to a screeching halt as well.

She had time on her hands and didn't know what to do with it. What had brought her joy and meaning for decades was all gone. Was her life over? Her husband didn't have time to fill the void because his life continued clicking along like it always had. Sure, he missed the boys too, but it was different for him. He hadn't made their meals, driven their car pools, signed the school forms, planned their birthdays, and everything else that goes with active parenting. Barbara was completely lost.

Barbara's story is similar to that of many mid-life women I know and have worked with. They have a vision for their life when they're young women, and they make that vision a reality. Then, somewhere along the path, they start to disappear in their own life behind the veil of loving other people, organizations, companies, or whatever their life is made up of. But by the time they get to mid-life, they realize this isn't a sustainable plan.

They're exhausted, and possibly even resentful that they've been giving everything for so long, forgetting themselves. Through that neglect, they've likely let their bodies go on some level, so their health may be compromised. With perimenopause, menopause, and postmenopause lasting a decade or longer, their emotions, sleeplessness, hot flashes, weight gain, and other "changes" have driven them crazy too and made them less than easy to be around at times. All of this can add up to relationship upheaval, professional upheaval, health upheaval, financial upheaval, and on and on and on. Life as they once knew it feels over. And they are terrified.

It Doesn't Have to Be This Way (Thank Goodness!)

The transformation solution I created is what I now call "The Mid-Life Makeover Method." Essentially, it includes six major shifts to address in your life that awaken you to your own patterns, help you identify what you want, help you get rid of what you don't want, and teach you how to think and act differently so you can be happier than ever. I did this work myself, and now I teach this to women everywhere in my talks, workshops, online courses, and coaching programs. If you choose to make a full commitment to this work, I guarantee you will be able to love yourself fully and live on your terms. It's time to make the middle years of your life the best years of your life so far!

Take Paula for example. When Paula first joined my coaching program, she was running her own company, but her customers were running her. She allowed them to tell her how to do her job. For years, she did everything but chop her head off to please these people—not getting paid what she was worth, working way too many hours, being harassed regularly, and taking care of duties not even in her job description.

Working through The Mid-Life Makeover Method in our coaching sessions changed everything. I helped Paula see how her own approach to business was actually exhausting her. I taught her how to speak confidently with her customers and put boundaries around her time, energy, and money. She got her finances in order, fired customers who did not treat her properly, and clearly defined her role in the company and the services she would provide. Together, we created a new vision for her life, personally and professionally. She was able to eliminate habits that were keeping her from living fully. Having learned to truly love herself, she now works less than full-time and makes more money. She enjoys her hobbies, spending time with her grandchildren, and traveling more. She is happier than she's ever been!

Then there's Michelle. After a divorce, she found herself alone, tired, lost, and ready for a career change. Thrown by her long marriage ending, Michelle didn't really know what she wanted or needed anymore. She just knew her life wasn't working. After attending one of my workshops, she joined my coaching program and started giving herself a makeover with The Mid-Life Makeover Method. She was able to take a good, hard look at herself and how toxic her relationships were. She realized she had been *over*-giving and *over*-functioning with her spouse, family, and friends.

She spent time really considering what she wanted her life to look like personally and professionally. She acknowledged that she wanted and needed a fresh start. She started to consider what would be life-giving to her instead of focusing on what others expected of her. After getting clear about this, she moved to a community that better suited her and gave her some much-needed space from the toxic people in her life. She chose to be trained in another field and now loves her new profession. She's adopted animals, loves to go hiking, and spends time traveling. She's made new friends and is truly loving her life and herself!

Terri gave her life to her children, and they got really used to that. Everything was about them, so when they left after high school, she was devastated and lost. Even though her marriage was intact, the change in her role as a mother was almost too much to bear. Who was she now without the kids around to dote on? She hadn't done anything for herself in decades. She hadn't given her own needs a second thought in so long that she hardly knew what she wanted for lunch, let alone how to build a life of her own.

She came to me for help. We walked through The Mid-Life Makeover Method step-by-step, and she started to understand that she was an individual, with hopes and dreams of her own, long before she ever became a mother. She reconnected with some of her old passions, found new things to try, and built a new daily life filled with meaningful activities and more fun than she's had in years. She's also been able to redefine her relationships with her young-adult children. They've created new habits of communication and new traditions as a family. This has been a healthy shift for all of them.

As she has learned to love herself more and shifted her priorities, her relationship with her husband has also grown. They schedule regular dinner dates and have joined a pickleball group together. He supports the work she's doing at the local homeless shelter by occasionally volunteering with her and by attending fundraising events. They're finding their "new normal" together in the empty nest.

No matter where you've been, what you're going through now, or how desperate you feel, I promise that when you give yourself a proper makeover from the inside out by applying everything in The Mid-Life Makeover Method, you can love yourself fully and live on your terms. Mid-life can become the best and happiest years of your life so far!

The Ripple Effect

The beauty of all of this is what's possible not just for you but for everyone around you. When you learn to put yourself first and to honor who you are and what you want and need, it's a game-changer for everyone! Let me explain.

You cannot give what you do not have. If someone needs an orange and you don't have one, you can't provide it. If you don't love and appreciate yourself, you cannot truly love and appreciate others. However, when you make yourself a priority and have filled your cup to overflowing, you will have much more to give to those you wish to serve. No longer running on empty, you will show up in your relationships content, happy, and fulfilled. You will be more fun to be around. You will be more interesting to talk to. You will not be giving to others with the last ounce of gumption you can muster.

You will also be modeling how to be an awesome woman! You will be teaching by example how to respectfully say no to opportunities that don't fit you. You will demonstrate diving into the things you truly value with a deep passion. In living your newly balanced life, you can easily prioritize the people and experiences most important to you, and those in your circles will feel the benefit of this. They will be attracted to your energy and delight in being around you.

The confidence and grace you'll exude will captivate them, and they will bask in your presence, which will cause them to raise the bar in their own lives. By being yourself, you will inspire others to reach their highest potential. The more people you can affect in this way, the wider the ripple will expand and the potential for greatness everywhere grows and grows. Never forget, you are part of something bigger than yourself, and you always have been. As an author, poet, and entertainer, Maya Angelou once said to Oprah Winfrey, "Your legacy is every life you touch."

The problem is that many women believe it's in everyone else's best interest for them to sacrifice their own needs and wants in order to give to others. For generations, young girls have directly witnessed the women in their families doing this. Stop and think for a moment about the roles your mothers and grandmothers played in their families. Holiday after holiday, I watched my mother, aunts, and grandmothers slave away in the kitchen for hours, preparing elaborate meals for everyone while the men sat in the living room, watching sports and exchanging stories. Then the women would serve the meal and do all the cleanup work as well, while the men went back to their comfortable recliners or outside for a cigar.

This is just one tiny example of a powerful message that women are supposed to give themselves up in the name of caring for others. Not that I ever heard any of them complaining, actually. I think it was what was modeled to them, so they continued the pattern. This strong message led our generation to think we were also doing the right thing in forgetting about ourselves and focusing on everyone else. Little did we know we were actually depriving not only ourselves but others in the process.

Other common examples of this include women being the ones to quit their jobs to raise their children, the family moving to accommodate the men's career aspirations, men being the primary breadwinners and decision-makers, and women in our generation feeling obligated to juggle everything—raising the children, managing all the domestic responsibilities, *and* working full-time outside the home to bring in additional financial support for the family.

The truth is—and there is evidence of this in every arena of life—when women treat themselves with high regard, make themselves a priority, feel good about themselves, and go for everything they want, everyone wins! What's best for women is best for all.

Women's relationships will be enhanced by their newfound balance. They will show up more honestly and authentically. They will be happier and healthier, which adds to the delight, joy, and experiences of those around them. As these women's self-love and confidence grow, they will see how they are powerful influencers and role models. Their self-respect will command the respect of others, so they will be taken more seriously. As women take action on the things that matter most to them (and stop wasting time doing things that don't), their energy levels will rise and their impact will be greater than it's ever been. Who doesn't benefit from being in the direct path of someone with this level of joy and satisfaction?

So, doing a mid-life makeover for yourself is actually an act of love and service far beyond the boundaries of your own life. Everyone that you come in contact with will experience a different energy around you and will be drawn to you. Your legacy will become one of how to live an awesome, meaningful life. You will demonstrate firsthand the joys of being a woman who has become happier, healthier, wealthier, and wiser in every way—even as she ages.

Chapter Two

Dropping the Bomb

It was now late October, and there was a chill in the air. Over a month had passed since my conversation with my husband in our van. Nothing new had happened during that time that had swayed my decision that divorce was imminent. I had continued praying, meditating, and going to therapy to make sure I was doing the best thing. I had contacted a lawyer to better understand, from a legal standpoint, what was at stake if I left the marriage. All roads had led me to this moment. I knew I needed to tell my husband I was going to divorce him.

Why did I choose bedtime on a Wednesday in October to drop the bomb? I don't remember. I just remember being conscious of the fact that our daughter's birthday was in September and our son's was in November, and I didn't want them to associate this traumatic life change with their birthday months. I suppose I thought it was smart to tell him when the kids were in bed and we were at the end of another day of responsibilities ourselves. I don't know. There's no good time to break someone's heart, especially someone you've loved for so long. Yet, I knew I could no longer remain and stay sane.

He was in our bed, awake, and I sat next to him. I told him that every month for the past year, I'd asked him to join me in working on our marriage. I'd pointed out the key areas I felt we needed help with to be able to continue to be together. I'd made it very clear that if he did not join me in relationship work in some form or another, I would divorce him. I explained that every time I'd brought this up, he'd insisted we were fine and then questioned why I was trying to cause us trouble. Finally, I said, "You have consistently shown me your unwillingness to work on our marriage and your total disregard for what's important to me. So, I *am* going to divorce you."

He began crying immediately and begged me to reconsider. I told him I already had a lawyer. He asked me to please hold off telling anyone or filing. He asked me to give him some time. I'd already given him all kinds of time—twenty-two years of marriage to be exact, plus the years we dated before we got married. Then there were all the times throughout the years that I'd asked him to seek help with me *and* the monthly requests for the past year with the divorce threat right there in front of him every time.

He didn't want this. Of course, I didn't either, really. I wanted to be happy, to feel healthy, to find myself again, and I just couldn't figure out how to do that in the context of the marriage. Over the years, my life had become consumed with what he wanted, needed, and thought was important. Many of our priorities were the same, but any time I had an idea, a thought, or a feeling that did not align in his mind, he would tell me it was wrong. I should be thinking this way, not that way, feeling this way, not that way. Whenever there were two options before us, we did what he was comfortable with. My individuality had disappeared. I felt like I was a nonfactor in my marriage and my life. Furthermore, his out-of-control temper was too much for me to bear any longer.

When I imagined staying, my life was very predictable. I would remain in the same small town for the rest of my life. I would spend every holiday in the same place. I would continue to be a therapist, working for other people. I would do the same church work I'd done for years. I would likely be lonely in my own house, continue to be degraded for my wants and needs, and never pursue my own personal or professional dreams. In a few short years, the kids would be gone, and then my husband and I would be living our parallel lives with almost nothing in common anymore. I could see myself spiraling even further.

However, if I left, I could build a life based on my own ideas, thoughts, and feelings. I could take complete responsibility for myself and the details of how I lived. I didn't know what that would look like exactly, but at least I would only have myself to blame, no matter what happened. And I became willing to take the risk for the open-ended possibilities of it all.

So, even though I felt like I was doing the unthinkable, I also felt like I was going to come back to life. Makeovers aren't necessarily easy, that's for sure, but they are worth it. I was worth it. You are worth it.

Leaving my marriage was the ultimate act of taking total responsibility for my life. It was the first major step of many in my mid-life makeover. Over the next several years, my makeover involved learning how to love myself like never before, building unwavering confidence, and making my needs a priority at last. At the same time, I adjusted to an empty nest, managed my grief over my father's sudden death (and handling his estate), helped attend to my elderly grandparents, and eventually took a professional sabbatical in order to relocate and start my own business. Learning how to date again and create a healthy partnership also became part of the picture. My relationship with my body continues to evolve, as does my spiritual growth.

Your makeover may not be nearly as dramatic as mine, but I bet you can relate to some of this, right? Or perhaps your tangible changes will be even more drastic! The main ingredient required for a successful makeover, no matter what form it takes on the outside, is learning to love yourself fully and taking complete responsibility for your happiness, period. That's it. It's up to you!

Is This You?

You're probably wondering, *Who am I now? What happened to me? Is this all there is? Is it too late for me?* These questions may even be the reasons you picked up this book. I understand this so much.

The longer you focus on what you thought you were supposed to do and fill the roles you think you are supposed to fill, the lower your life satisfaction level falls. And isn't it interesting how much we loved those roles, how driven we were to do them well, and how quickly we lost ourselves in the process?

You are not alone. I have been there, as have millions of other women. In reaching mid-life, you find yourself asking powerful questions you haven't had a moment to ask before because you've been consumed with managing a household, raising children, trying to keep your marriage thriving, and running a company on top of it! Then there are all the thousand other things you've been doing—helping at the school, serving at the church, organizing the neighborhood activities, sitting on community boards, volunteering here and there, balancing the budget, hosting gatherings for your friends and family, and on and on and on it goes!

I'm with you, sister! One-hundred-percent!

Let's go back to those core questions for a moment. Here are my quick answers to them:

- *Who am I now?* You are a loving, beautiful, individual soul with thoughts, feelings, needs, and wants unique to you.

- *What happened to me?* You consumed yourself with loving and serving others, not realizing that, at the same time, you were neglecting a part of yourself that was bigger than the roles you were playing.

- *Is this all there is?* No, it's not. The possibilities are endless for you!

- *Is it too late for me?* Only if you decide it is. If you want your life to be different, you can make it different. You can keep as much of it the same as you see fit, even while you're making changes that feel good, honest, and important to you.

Remember, you are responsible for your own happiness. No one else. No one.

The Bigger Answer

When you enter the mid-life zone and find yourself unhappy, you are likely to look outside yourself for answers. You could easily find blame in your childhood upbringing, the bosses who have treated you unfairly, the partners who have abused you or left you, the friends who have abandoned you, the children who don't appreciate you, your crazy family members, the doctors who didn't diagnose you properly, the church, the school, the neighborhood, the community, the government, the economy, the state of the world—you fill in the blank.

The problem is that even though other people, places, organizations, and entities affect your life, at the end of the day, blaming them does you no good. When you blame other people or circumstances for your dissatisfaction or turmoil—even when you are certain they deserve it—you are giving your power away, which only leaves you feeling more helpless, hopeless, and depressed.

The Mid-Life Makeover Method empowers you in every area of your life. You don't have to rely on others to change in order to get where you want to go.

You take charge of yourself and your circumstances in every way. You do this by engaging in six major shifts.

The Six Shifts

First and foremost, you have to wake up! Yes, wake up from the deep sleep of not being real with yourself. Waking up means *big-time* self-awareness—recognizing who you really are, the roles you've played, how you've shown up in your life and your relationships, what you're doing that works well, and what you're doing that doesn't work. It's about assessing the damage as well as how this has affected those around you.

Second, you need to get crystal clear about what you want. Without clarity, you cannot create anything. In every area of your life, you must ask yourself the powerful question, *What do you wish for, long for, and desire?* Without a solid vision for your life, you will remain directionless.

Third, you need to eliminate energy drainers. Energy drainers are anything you no longer want, need, or use. Simplifying, decluttering, and organizing are involved as well as fixing your messes and incomplete projects, which makes your life work more efficiently. Essentially, this involves letting go of anyone or anything that no longer aligns with your life or the vision you have for your future.

Fourth, you must master your mindset. Your mind can either be your worst enemy or your best friend. You will learn how to identify the limiting beliefs that have run your life so far and how to replace them to create the life you really want. You will stop all negative self-talk and dismantle your worries and fears. You will understand what I call your "T.F.A. Cycle"—how your thoughts lead to your feelings, which lead to your actions—and how to change any scenario to lead you to a path of greater joy and satisfaction.

Fifth, you will develop success habits, such as writing specific goals and incorporating new daily routines that support you in getting where you want to go. You will drop old habits that no longer serve you, which will free you to create a life of greater joy and meaning.

Sixth, and lastly, equipped with a strong support system, you will develop a sustainability plan, investing in yourself in every way you need to keep up your momentum and carry yourself into the rest of your life. You will step into the role of being the leader in your own life and never look back at your old ways of doing things, where you got lost in the shuffle of your former priorities.

The Mid-Life Makeover Method provides the path to letting go of your "old story" and writing the "new story" of your life. You will learn how to love yourself fully and live on your terms. You can make mid-life the best, happiest years of your life while building the confidence to move forward into the future feeling better than ever!

Chapter Three

The Path of Self-Discovery

As a therapist and coach working with people to improve their lives, I've found myself teaching the same concepts over and over again. Throughout my life, I've also read tons of self-help books, attended several trainings on ways to help people, and gone through my own transformation.

When I entered mid-life and realized my life satisfaction was plummeting, I knew I needed to find the best ways to cope and evolve so I could be happy. My journey continued with extensive training with Jack Canfield, author of the *Chicken Soup for the Soul*® book series and *The Success Principles*™. This intensive study, along with my years of experiences with clients, led me to identify the core shifts required for someone to change their life holistically. I began testing different approaches with my clients and found the elements of these core shifts that accomplished the greatest results for anyone with any issue.

The Mid-Life Makeover Method was born. Shifting your life by looking at it from the inside out, instead of the outside in, catapults your ability to create changes right away. Before people understand this, they waste time looking outside of themselves for people or circumstances to blame, then expect the other people or circumstances to change while they sit back and wait to benefit. This is a backward approach.

When you start by looking straight at yourself, honestly and willingly, you set yourself up for much greater success—and much more quickly as well! You own your life, your thoughts, your choices, and your decisions, *and* you uncover the patterns that have gotten you where you are right now. Then you have something to build on. All that opportunity is lost if you just look to others for your answers. You must become the leader of your own life.

Here are some key questions to get you started on the path of self-discovery:

- Who am I?

- How have I shown up to arrive at this point in my life?

- What are my strengths? Where do I need to grow?

- What do I like about myself? What don't I like?

I'm sure you can see the value in asking yourself these questions as a starting point. You must be willing to be very honest with yourself though, or the process won't work.

Let's talk about Julia for a moment. Julia was in the process of divorce number four. She was so loving and devoted to every man she'd loved and was, therefore, baffled by the repeated failed marriages. She gave fully, loved fully, and had sacrificed much of herself in the name of love over the years.

When she began using The Mid-Life Makeover Method and asked herself these powerful questions in the safety of working with her coach (me!), she began to see how she had shown up in the journey of picking her husbands. She began to see how quickly she could trust a sweet-talking man, fall in love with him, give up the other aspects of her life, and become his everything. She also realized how quick she was to overlook bad behavior or warning signs. She was also very willing to justify and forgive dishonest behavior and other less-than-honorable aspects of the men in her life just to have love and "be loved."

Through her coaching, she realized how her ability to love was a strength but also how her tendency to jump quickly into a serious relationship was counterproductive. She learned new ways of showing up in the dating world and built her confidence up, which led her standards to be much higher in terms of the kinds of men she was willing to have dinner with, let alone marry. She learned to love and appreciate herself so much that she did not need a man to "feed" her any longer. She learned to fill her own cup to overflowing and allowed her romantic relationships and experiences to simply become a fun accessory in her life instead of a strong mission to "get a man."

Then there's Melinda, who was struggling in her relationships with her two young-adult daughters. The empty nest had been a very difficult transition for her. She was very accustomed to controlling her girls' lives. Shortly after they both left home, her daughters became less and less communicative. They did not return every text or call and rarely came home. This left Melinda distraught and concerned. She sought my help to sort through the situation.

Tempted to blame her daughters for simply wanting to "spread their wings," Melinda had trouble seeing how her own behavior had alienated them. When she dove into The Mid-Life Makeover Method and began honestly looking at her own role in the relationships, she saw how she had smothered her girls, albeit from a place of love and protectiveness for them. She could finally see how badly they needed the chance to make their own decisions and experience some self-responsibility in their lives. She also became secure enough with herself to not define her life based on how much or how little she heard from or saw her daughters. She got a life of her own outside of motherhood.

All of this, of course, changed the dynamics between them and led them to come together again in a way that was balanced and healthy for everyone. Melinda has found new joy in life by volunteering at the local hospital and starting her own book club. The girls continue to thrive as young women, establishing their careers, and they now look forward to spending time with their mother.

If Julia or Melinda had not been willing to examine themselves thoroughly by asking these key questions, none of the transformations in their lives and relationships with themselves or others would have been possible.

When you're willing to do so as well, you'll have a strong start for your own makeover. I know it's not always easy to see yourself and your role in your own life and circumstances, but once you can, with your eyes and your mind wide open, anything is possible.

You can see what has worked and what hasn't. You can tease out the habits you have that cause you distress and select new patterns that support what you want. Back that up with a new and healthy mindset, and you're off and running!

Eventually, you will truly love yourself fully and live on your terms. Mid-life then becomes the best and happiest time of your life instead of the season of turmoil it started out as.

I Know What You're Thinking...

This all sounds great to you in theory, I'm sure. But I can imagine what you're thinking right about now because I hear these things all the time from women facing their own crises in mid-life.

1. *It's too late for me.*

When did you get it into your head that when you reach the age of forty, fifty, or even sixty that your time is up? Women say this to me *all the time*, whether it's about getting their health in order, their finances fixed, finding love again, pursuing a meaningful career, or even learning something new!

Do you realize you might only be halfway through your life at this point? Halfway! Not two steps from death. It is only too late for you if you *believe* it is. Think of all the women you've heard of who have done remarkable things well into their seventies, eighties, and nineties. Women have run marathons, started nonprofit organizations, begun entirely new careers, gotten married again, and won awards for service or inventions. Not to mention the "easier" accomplishments like flying in an airplane for the first time, learning a new language, joining a yoga class, or going back to college.

2. *I'm too old to change. I'm stuck in my ways.*

You may very well be "stuck in your ways," and that is one of the problems that can be addressed. Are your ways working for you? If you're not happy and wildly satisfied with your life, then they're not. If you're stuck, you can become unstuck. But you have to be willing to try new things. That's the only requirement to start nudging yourself in a new direction: honesty and willingness. Are you honest? Are you willing? Then you are not too old to change your ways.

3. *It's someone else's fault.*

Yes, others play a part in your world. Other people are going to do what they are going to do and say what they are going to say. You cannot control them. You cannot change them. You can invite their participation in the evolution of your relationship, but at the end of the day, they will need to want to change in order to join you in that process. (Remember my husband?)

So, you can continue to focus on everything "they" have done or not done or how you are a victim in your own life, but that will get you nowhere but more miserable and completely stuck. Again, your true power lies in your ability to take a serious look at what you are doing and not doing that works or does not work in getting you the life you really want. It's not about blaming yourself, either. It's about taking charge of yourself and becoming a leader in your own life without letting other people, events, or "realities" take charge of you.

4. I've never done anything like this before.

No, you probably haven't. If you want different results in your life, you're going to have to try new approaches to living, thinking, believing, and behaving. You won't have to change everything, and you can pace yourself by building up your comfort level with change over time. Rome wasn't built in a day, and your life doesn't need to be either.

It's all about choices. Trying something new may turn out to be the best thing you've ever done. You may find whole new levels of joy, meaning, delight, stimulation, excitement, happiness, and health. You don't know what you don't know. Your life is likely to continue to be much the same if you don't do something different. Are you willing to keep going down this path for another ten, twenty, thirty, or more years? Is it worth avoiding the worry or fear around doing something different? What's the worst that could happen if you try?

5. It's not that bad, really.

This is my favorite. This is classic human behavior. You know you're miserable. You know you're lost. You know life doesn't have to be this awful. You've admitted all of this. You have sought answers. You have an opportunity to regroup, heal, grow, change, and find a better life for yourself. But then, you stop. You freeze. You decide life's not that bad after all. You've exaggerated. You were just hormonal. People are starving in other countries; your life is easy compared to that. So-and-so is far worse off than you, so you decide to just stop complaining and accept the status quo.

I call this "the disease of mediocrity"—settling for a life that is unhappy and unfulfilled. And there's no good reason for that! Not for anyone. Mid-life is often full of turmoil and challenges you never imagined possible. I get how overwhelming this can be. But telling yourself that it's no big deal is like watching your home burn to the ground with everyone you love in it and saying, "Oh well."

Through years of slowly losing track of yourself, your normal temperature has changed, so to speak, and you may not remember what it feels like to feel really good. You may have completely lost touch with what sincere joy and satisfaction feel like, so "not so bad" is a skewed version of what's really happening. The cost of this kind of denial is incredible.

The Cost

Continuing down the path of resignation, stubbornness, blame, fear, and denial will only add to the negative symptoms you're experiencing. If you're depressed, you will get more depressed. If you're stressed, you will get more stressed. If you have pain, this will likely increase and may become chronic. If you struggle to manage your finances, your financial security will continue to be increasingly compromised.

Your relationships will remain challenged and unsatisfying. The distance between you and your loved ones will become wider. The ambivalence you feel will grow stronger. The abuse or neglect may increase. Your loneliness will be more profound. Conflict will rise. Communication will suffer. You may find yourself turning to unhealthy choices to find some relief, connectedness, or control. This never works.

Your days, weeks, months, and years will pile onto one another like bricks on your shoulders, with only aging there to remind you of the time you're wasting. The healthy people around you who want more for you will watch in horror as you let your life pass you by. They will become frustrated or disillusioned with you. They may even need to disconnect due to the hopelessness they feel when trying to encourage you to live more fully.

Is this *really* what you want? To be a victim of your past, stuck in your present, with no future to look forward to at all? Do you want to keep abusing yourself by staying in the same place with the same attitude and the same self-destructive patterns?

What if it could be different? What if it didn't have to be this way at all? I *promise* you it doesn't. *It really does not!* I know the way out of all this. I've done it myself, and I've helped other women do it as well. You can begin today.

In the next few chapters we are going to dive deeper into the six major shifts of The Mid-Life Makeover Method. With each shift, I will explain the steps involved, you will meet a woman who has done the work herself with amazing results, and I will give you an opportunity to put this into practice on your own. Every chapter will present a chance for you to start your own makeover in different areas of your life. This is your new beginning. Just keep reading . . .

Chapter Four
Waking Up!

BEING WILLING TO TAKE AN HONEST LOOK AT YOURSELF AND HOW YOU'RE IMPACT-ing your own life is a critical first step in your makeover. I call this *waking up!*

Meet Jolene

Jolene was falling apart in her personal and professional life when she signed up for The 90-Day Mid-Life Makeover Private Coaching Program. Her husband had left her, her children were no longer speaking to her, and she was on probation at work. Everything important to her seemed to be crumbling.

There had been warning signs. Her boss had taken her into his office several times and told her she needed to get to work on time and be sober when she arrived. Her husband had threatened to leave many times as he dumped another bottle of wine down the drain in their kitchen. The children started coming home less and less for visits. Eventually, they stopped communicating with her completely because she ignored their requests to get help. Jolene was an alcoholic who was actively drinking and creating turmoil in every part of her life.

Together we worked through step one of The Mid-Life Makeover Method. Jolene started to see how her own choice to drink had alienated everyone in her life. She started to realize the damaging effect drinking was having on her relationships, her ability to be fully present for others, and her ability to function properly at work. Through her increase in self-awareness by asking the tough questions, Jolene could finally connect the dots between her behavior and the unfortunate consequences of that behavior.

Eventually, Jolene moved through all the steps of The Mid-Life Makeover Method, restored her relationships with her children, and found new ways to cope emotionally (instead of drinking). She has now been sober for two years, continues to attend Alcoholics Anonymous meetings regularly, and has kept her job. None of this would have been possible if she had not woken up.

Like Jolene, many people refuse to wake up in their lives until traumatic evidence presents itself. I find that many of my clients have to lose a lot before they get help. They seem stuck in victimhood, believing life is just happening *to* them. The truth is, when someone chooses not to wake up, they're giving their power away to other people and circumstances. When someone gets caught up in the blaming-and-complaining game, they're focusing outside of themselves and, therefore, cannot ignite any changes that would feel good to them. The results are devastating. My term for people who refuse to listen to how their lives are speaking to them and see their direct involvement in the results is "ostrich."

Ostriches are known for sticking their heads in the sand. When they do so, they cannot see or hear what's going on around them. They are also choosing to be stuck and not take any action. They leave themselves vulnerable to predators who could do them harm. Anything could go wrong at any moment because the ostrich isn't paying attention and is, therefore, "asleep" in their life, not taking a good look at the reality of how their choices are creating their troubles. Unless the ostrich chooses to wake up, take its head out of the sand, and get actively involved in the trajectory of its life, it will remain a victim to it. Are you an ostrich?

If so, it's time to take your head out of the sand and take a good, long look in the mirror. Ask yourself these powerful questions:

- What's working in my life? What's not working?

- What am I pretending to not know?

- How am I affecting those around me?

- What strengths or qualities do I have that have led to joy in my life?

- What changes would I like to make within myself?

- If I were to be my most authentic self, what would that look like?

Your answers to these powerful questions will lead you to several important aspects of your mid-life makeover.

First, you will realize how your choices and behaviors have led to your current circumstances, for better or for worse. This is valuable insight. Take note. Then, you will have a sense of how you really feel about yourself, your character, your strengths, and your areas for growth. Next, you will begin to form a vision of who you would like to be and how you would like to show up in your life from this point forward. Finally, and perhaps most importantly, you will shift your focus from people and circumstances outside of yourself to look inward instead, taking responsibility for your life and happiness where your power truly lies.

When I Woke Up

When I "woke up" in my midforties, although I didn't like realizing how I had caused several of my own struggles, I felt empowered to change and finally let go of the helplessness and hopelessness attached to waiting on someone else to make my life better. For me, waking up involved realizing I was the common denominator of all my problems. When I looked carefully at my own behavior, I saw how I had created a pattern of saying yes to every request, whether I felt capable of adding it to my plate or not. I realized I was allowing myself to be treated unfairly in my marriage and some of my other significant relationships. I kept tolerating unhealthy, toxic behavior from loved ones because I thought I had to.

Another pattern I had created in my life was consistently ignoring my own needs. I put my children and husband first, then my job, my church, the schools, my friends, and all the other organizations I was involved with. I wouldn't even let myself read for pleasure if someone else needed something. This is nothing to be proud of, trust me. By the time I entered everyone else's schedules into my calendar, there wasn't any space left for me. I was also over-functioning at work, letting team members and board members under-function and get away with it. This list goes on and on about how I created my own storm.

What I found to be true for myself is also the truth for many women who seek my help. Our self-love is compromised or nonexistent. Part of the waking up step is assessing how you feel about yourself. The reality is, when we do not fully love ourselves, we do not make ourselves a priority, and then we let other people and things become more important, which in turn creates an imbalance of our priorities, time, energy, and resources.

This is exactly the reason our makeover is *from the inside out,* not the other way around. To get to the tangible changes in your life—whether it's healing a relationship, improving your health, or getting out of debt—you must first learn to properly love yourself, recognize your worth, and build your own terms for life. Then you can manifest the tangible results from a place of greater love and confidence.

Thank goodness I became miserable enough to start asking myself the tough questions and admitting my own role and responsibility in my circumstances. Again, waking up and being real with yourself isn't easy. For most of my coaching clients, this is a very difficult step. However, once someone is willing to do it, it's very empowering! Just like for me, my clients' self-love had to grow first and *then* they could create outer results that felt better. They could focus on their strengths, take action, and stop waiting for someone or something else to change.

As I learned to love myself fully, I stopped criticizing myself and those around me so much. I stopped overworking. I started engaging in things that mattered to me, such as personal development, traveling, and spending time with friends. I began meditating and seeing a therapist to help me heal and grow. I said no when I needed to for my health and well-being. And that was just the tip of the iceberg for me and my makeover.

The Possibilities Are Endless

What about you? What if you loved yourself more this year than you ever have before? What might that feel like on the inside and how would it manifest on the outside? The possibilities are endless!

When you ask yourself, *Who do I think I am?* what comes up for you? Maybe you attach your identity to the roles you play in your relationships. Maybe you identify most with your profession. Maybe you believe you are your body, your money, or your belief system. Waking up is having a solid understanding of who you think you are and how you feel about yourself.

From there, ask yourself, *What is working well in my life?* Maybe you have the health you want. Perhaps you are in a very loving marriage that has lasted for decades. Maybe you just got promoted at work with a nice raise attached. Maybe you've learned how to speak a new language and have international travel planned.

Knowing what's working well in your life is very important because it's a confidence-building piece that offers you clues about the strengths, qualities, and skills you already have that can be applied to other areas of your life. So, think about that. What qualities, skills, and strengths have you been utilizing to create success in the areas you indicated above?

Maybe you're healthy because you're very good at preparing nutritious meals for yourself and keeping a consistent exercise routine. Maybe you're in a lasting marriage because you have strong communication skills. Maybe you're professionally successful because you're very organized, you're approachable, and you provide your customers with the necessary information and products in a timely manner.

When you begin to expand your self-awareness to areas that aren't working, you may be able to come back to these strengths and utilize them to turn your situation around elsewhere. For example, you may be struggling financially and have mounting debt. How could you use the strengths you already possess to fix your money issues?

Your organizational skills could be used to create a budget. Your ability to establish healthy food and exercise routines could be transferred into routine spending and saving with appropriate boundaries to pay your bills in a timely manner and chip away at the debt more quickly. Your communication skills could be utilized in your relationships with your bankers, financial advisors, and creditors so that everyone has your goals in mind and is on the same page with your plan.

When assessing what's not working, you want to include an honest reflection about the damaging effects of your behavior on others. Just like Jolene, if you're actively drinking too much, you may be alienating your children. They may feel unable to count on their mother because you're emotionally unavailable due to your alcohol consumption.

Then there's my former coworker Melinda, who regularly showed up late for staff meetings. She seemed to have no regard for anyone else on the team. This total lack of awareness of how she affected others led to frustration from the rest of us as meetings often ran late because we had to wait for her to start. This did not serve the team's effectiveness or morale, and she lost our respect in many ways.

In relationships, whether personal or professional, it's critical that you understand how you're showing up both effectively and ineffectively. Acting like the ostrich will only get you in deeper trouble than facing the music of what's really going on.

Most women I work with are scared to make an honest assessment of their part in the life they have. Denial keeps reality at bay, and this is partially why so many women end up unhappy by the time they get to the middle of their lives. They know something is off, maybe way off, but they're clueless as to how it all happened.

What's Your Self-Esteem Score?

When things aren't working well, your self-esteem suffers, even if you blame other people or events for the situation. Your self-esteem is basically how you feel about yourself, and understanding this is a critical piece of waking up because your self-esteem determines how you're going to show up in your life and whether you will feel empowered to change or not. Do you know how you feel about yourself? Think for a moment. On a scale of zero (you don't love yourself at all) to ten (you are happy as heck with yourself), where do you land?

Let's say your number is a three. You're not feeling great about yourself. Now, look at the thoughts that accompany the number. Maybe you say things to yourself like, *I'm a failure. I'm not as young/thin/sharp as I used to be. I'm stupid. I can't do anything right. I'm tired, old, fat, and lost.*

If your number is an eight, you may have thoughts like, *I'm strong. I can do anything I set my mind to. I like and appreciate myself.* Good for you! How you feel about yourself is a key piece in living fully, being happier than you've ever been, and making this the best time of your life so far!

No matter what self-esteem score you chose, you have begun the waking up process just by being aware of it. As you ask the other powerful questions in this step, you will be able to see how your self-esteem directly affects what's working and what's not working in your life. You'll be able to connect the relationship your self-esteem level has with the results you're getting in your life.

This is powerful information you can utilize as you move through the rest of The Mid-Life Makeover Method.

Find Your Vision

The last part of waking up is to use your imagination to visualize, in detail, what you believe would be possible for you if you were to take full responsibility for your life. Try your best to examine how the path of your life could be different if you loved yourself fully and did not let anything stop you from going after everything important to you.

As you continue with your makeover, having a vision for what you want your life to look like will be very important. The waking up step helps us look at the roles we've played in getting us to where we are today, and it also helps us see where we could go from here should we desire to. I want you to develop a possibility consciousness, where you open your mind wider to what life could look like, sound like, and feel like. You may really need to stretch yourself here and expand your ideas of what a fulfilling life might include.

If you don't *choose* to wake up, you'll never know what this fulfilling life could be. Guaranteed.

Key Takeaways

- Your happiness depends on waking up!
- Blaming and complaining about people and events is a waste of time and takes your power away.
- Knowing who you are and how you feel about yourself is the beginning of your mid-life makeover.
- Strengths and qualities you have that work well in one area of your life will help with your mid-life makeover in other areas of your life.
- What's not working in your life not only negatively affects you but others around you as well.
- Self-esteem is another key ingredient that affects the state of your mid-life makeover.
- Imagining and visualizing the possibilities will lead you into step two of your mid-life makeover.

Now, It's Your Turn: "Mirror, Mirror on the Wall"

Carve out some quiet time to spend looking in a mirror asking yourself these questions:

- Who am I?
- What's working in my life?
- What's not working in my life?
- What strengths do I have?
- What areas do I want to improve in?
- What would my life look like if I loved myself more this year than ever before?
- What would happen if I chose to take full responsibility for my life starting right now?

Journal your answers. When you want to skip a question, remind yourself that to love yourself fully means being honest with yourself first and foremost and that if you're going to live on your terms, you're going to have to find out where you are right now in relation to that.

Coming Up Next . . .

In the next chapter, you'll take everything you discovered as you woke up and get crystal clear about everything you want in your life. You'll be able to declare, in detail, what's most important for you to have in five key areas of your life. This is a critical piece of your mid-life makeover because you cannot get something if you don't know what it is.

Chapter Five

Getting Crystal Clear

Two weeks after I told my husband I was going to divorce him, I officially filed. One of the hardest parts of this whole experience was my own inner turmoil. I held a deep respect for the sanctity of marriage, for the lifelong commitment attached to it "no matter what," and had honestly intended to keep the "forever" promises I made that day.

And divorce? Well, I wasn't a big fan. My parents' divorce when I was thirteen years old set off one of the most traumatic, difficult stretches of my life, filled with grief, sadness, frustration, confusion, fear, worry, and anger. I had sworn up and down I would never put anybody through such a nightmare.

Yet, there I was, meeting with my newly hired lawyer, discussing what steps needed to be taken to end my twenty-two-year marriage. Ugh. My husband and I had two kids, ages sixteen and fourteen, who would inherit this transition whether they liked it or not. How could I be so selfish?

On the other hand, what good was I going to be to our children, my husband, or anyone if I continued to spiral and deny myself the life I truly wanted? Yes, I wanted to be married, but not like this. To me, marriage was to be an equal partnership, with your spouse being your greatest ally in life, your safe place to land. My marriage was none of these things—in many ways, it was the exact opposite. That's not marriage by my definition.

So even though I felt like I was doing the unthinkable, at the same time, I felt like I was coming back to life. The intensity of grief I felt, the sense of failure, the unknowns before me—they all greeted me every day. However, a hope for a brighter future, a more peaceful daily life, and the opportunity to live without restrictions entered the picture as well.

I wanted to wake up every morning feeling happy, calm, and excited for what the day may bring. I wanted to feel good more often than not, in every single way. I wanted to be emotionally available to my friends, family, clients, and colleagues, more so than I had been for quite some time. I didn't want to feel like I was hiding behind a facade of happiness and success. I wanted to live out my *own* definition of happiness and success—with gratitude and joy. I wanted my own coaching practice, and I wanted to spend more time with people who valued personal and professional development work. I wanted to be an amazing role model to my two children as someone who lived authentically—taking full responsibility for her life and confidently going for everything she dreamed of.

When you don't know what you want, you cannot get it, create it, or find it. Getting crystal clear about what you wish for, long for, and dream of is the first step to getting it. So, once you've woken up to who you are and how you've shown up in your life, it's time to clarify exactly what you want your life to look like from this point on.

"I'll Have What She's Having"

Imagine going into a restaurant, sitting down at a table, and scanning the menu. The waiter comes up to you and asks, "What can I get for you tonight?" If you say, "I'm hungry, just bring me something to eat," the waiter will be confused, first of all, but they will also be put in the impossible position of pleasing you. With all the options in front of you, how is the waiter to know what you like, if you're allergic to anything, what you're in the mood for, or what your budget is?

Without your specific instructions, you're likely to end up with a meal you're unsatisfied with in some way. Maybe the dressing won't be correct, the meat won't be cooked to your liking, or the chosen vegetable will be one you dislike. Life is like this. If we do not get crystal clear about what we want, we are likely to end up dissatisfied with our circumstances. You don't want to leave any of this to chance.

Think about your ideal life. Ask yourself what you most want, need, or desire in your life. Do this without apology or restrictions. You have your own unique definition of success and happiness and what those look like in tangible form. As you contemplate what you want, resist the temptation to worry about what's possible for you, what's not possible for you, and how all of this will come about. Those details are not significant in this step (we'll get to them later).

To get your thoughts rolling, let's look at several different areas in your life.

Your Health

What would life look like if you were living your ideal healthy life? This could be your physical, mental, emotional, or even spiritual health. Maybe you believe a certain body size, cholesterol level, or eyesight ability equates to ideal health. Maybe you believe health equates to experiencing happiness every single day. Maybe you feel healthy when you meditate, pray, or chant on a regular basis. Take some time to really think about your definition of health. You might even think of people you know (or know of) who exemplify health from your perspective. What do these people have in common? What do they look like? How are they living their lives in terms of health?

Fifty-year-old Nina, a private coaching client of mine, wanted to lose twenty pounds and get off insulin. For her, this would mean she was healthy physically and, therefore, would also feel healthier emotionally. Once she got clear about this, she joined a gym and hired a personal trainer to help her lose the weight. She also hired a nutritionist to help her create an eating regimen that supported regulating her insulin. By getting clear and having specific, measurable goals, Nina was able to create exactly what she wanted. She lost thirty pounds and has kept it off, and (after clearing it with her doctor) no longer requires insulin. She is ecstatic she was able to make these changes. If she had not gotten clear, this would not have happened.

Your Relationships

Now, think about your relationships. You probably have a combination of family, friends, neighbors, colleagues, classmates, teams, employees, committees, organizations, clients, and social media followers. What do you want your relationships to look and feel like? What kind of people do you want to spend the most time with? What kinds of activities do you want to engage in with those people? What roles do you want to play in your relationships? What would be the most honest expression of your authenticity in your relationships with others?

Relationships are a particularly interesting subject because you likely have some relationships you feel you don't have any choice about. For example, if you're married and have in-laws, whether you like them or not, they are likely to be a part of your life as long as you're in that marriage. Or perhaps you work at a company with a colleague or two who you would be perfectly happy to never see again, but you are in the same department and, therefore, required to work together.

Even in these circumstances (and maybe *especially* in these circumstances), you can set your ideal high and strive to reach that standard. As they get to the end of their lives, most people rarely say they set their goals or standards too high or wish they had settled for less. Most wish they had set their standards higher and asked more of themselves, others, and life. Your "ideal" is what you want to focus on throughout your makeover. Remember, you're learning to live on your terms, so set them high!

The quality of your relationships can be a powerful ingredient in your ideal life, so be picky. When relationships are less than healthy, somewhat toxic, or even downright abusive, you should consider drastically reducing the amount of time you spend with those people or even cutting them out of your life altogether. Boundary setting is a powerful tool in managing the health of your relationships and your personal well-being.

Helen often struggled with the boundaries in her relationships. Helen's in-laws were a bit overbearing. They shared a business with all of their children, and although they no longer had their hands in the day-to-day operations of the company, they were never shy to share their opinions or give instructions on how things ought to be run. On top of this, they often communicated their opinions about how Helen and her siblings ought to be raising their children. Both of these things were taking their toll.

She wanted to learn from them, as they had run the family business for decades, but without receiving unsolicited advice so regularly. She wanted to enjoy personal time with them, have fun, and be together without business talk. She wanted her children to grow up appreciating and enjoying time with the older generation of their family.

When Helen and I started working together, we contemplated how best to create an ideal relationship with her in-laws despite the difficult dynamics she was experiencing. By using The Mid-Life Makeover Method, Helen learned how to reframe her thoughts about her in-laws (we'll dive into this in Mastering Your Mindset—stay tuned!) and how to define what would be an enjoyable and satisfying relationship with them.

One of the things Helen realized as she got clearer about her relationships was how much she appreciated the activities her in-laws provided for her children. She realized that the more time she allowed them to spend with her children, the happier they were and the less likely they were to judge her parenting. Meanwhile, the kids basked in the attention of their grandparents. This also gave Helen some much-needed "me" time. Everyone wins!

Through our coaching sessions, Helen learned how to respectfully respond to her in-laws' suggestions with gratitude while still feeling confident about her own choices and actions, ultimately making her own decisions about her life, her parenting, and the family business.

By building her confidence and learning new communication skills, she was also able to ask if their family dinners could be business-free and focused only on their personal lives. They agreed. The healthy boundaries Helen incorporated helped her create the ideal relationships with her in-laws that she'd always wanted.

You spend so much time in your relationships with others, in all kinds of settings. No matter what kind of relationships you consider during this makeover process, remember that there is an ideal for you to set. The clearer you are about it, the more likely you are to create this ideal. Although we cannot control other people's thoughts or behaviors, we can always control our own in any relationship. Setting a clear standard will direct you in all of your relationship encounters.

Your Finances

Another important area to get crystal clear about is your financial life. For some reason, money is a highly sensitive topic for most people. We are more likely to freely talk about religion, politics, sex, or just about anything than about our finances.

I'm not asking you to divulge your financial secrets. However, if you truly want to love yourself, live fully, and be happier than you've ever been, you'll need to get really clear about what you want in your financial life and take an honest assessment of where you currently are so you can bridge the gap between those two things.

In the area of finances, what would be ideal for you? How much money would you have in savings? How much income would you be bringing in every month? What would financial security look like to you? What kind of retirement package would you want in place? How much money would you be spending on your needs and wants every month? Would you be giving charitably, and if so, how much and to what organizations? What investments, property, or other symbols of wealth are important to you? These are all powerful, important questions to consider regarding your finances.

A former colleague of mine, Tanya, was married to Jeff. Jeff wanted to quit his job and take significant time off from his career. Tanya ran her own business with a fluctuating income and found Jeff's request quite unsettling. She asked me what I thought. We talked through what her ideal financial life would look like. Of all the things making her nervous, the biggest was the fear of losing their home if their financial life went awry. So, owning their home outright was the most important symbol of an ideal financial life for Tanya.

She shared this ideal with Jeff, who realized the only way for him to have his ideal (quitting his job) and for her to have her ideal (owning their home outright) was to take money out of their retirement fund to pay off the house. For both of them, this felt like a good solution. They could both breathe easier moving forward knowing Jeff could have his professional sabbatical and Tanya wouldn't fear losing their home.

Tanya and Jeff's example illustrates clearly that, though your ideal financial life may involve details that are very different from another person's, that doesn't make either of you wrong. At first, you may not know the specifics of how best to create your ideal financial life, but those details are not critical for this step of getting crystal clear. First, just get the vision. The details will show themselves as you move through your makeover.

Your Professional Life

Turn your eyes toward your professional life now. What I'm referring to as your professional life could encompass any of these things or others: a job; a career; a business; volunteerism; domestic responsibilities; caring for elderly parents; raising your children or grandchildren; or any other way you contribute to your family, neighborhood, community, the world, or society at large. Think of the areas in your life where you use your skills, qualities, training, education, and time to serve in some way.

What would be the ideal life for you professionally? When would you participate in this? What would you be doing? What kind of time commitment would
it involve? Is there compensation, and if so, what kind and how much? Are you
alone or working with others? Are you home or in a different setting? Whom
are you serving? What makes this profession satisfying, meaningful, and worth
all your efforts? What are you striving for? What do you want out of this area of
your life?

Johnna ran her own cleaning company for decades. She had happily served
hundreds of people by cleaning and organizing their homes. She had provided
jobs for many team members over the years. Her relationships with her clients,
colleagues, and customers were very satisfying.

However, when Johnna reached the middle of her life, things started to
change for her. She grew weary of coordinating so many schedules for employees and families. She was also beginning to feel the effects of the hard physical
labor on her body. Chronic pain and exhaustion were becoming regular issues.
She began to wonder how much longer this professional path would be realistic.

Johnna asked herself these powerful questions about what she would ideally like professionally at this point in her life. Having not worked at any other
job or for anyone else for nearly three decades, Johnna felt uncertain which
careers might be valid and possible for her. I encouraged her to just stay focused
on discovering what she wanted in an ideal situation instead of where or how
that could be found.

Johnna was able to identify these things as her ideal: a regular paycheck
with full benefits, no longer being her own boss, a commute of less than twenty
miles, no physically taxing tasks, helping others, and having coworkers she liked.
Once she got clear about those desires, she hired a recruiter to help her write a
solid resume and get interviews.

After only three months of diligent effort, Johnna landed a job that met all
of her criteria and more. She was able to shut down her business without any
guilt and begin a new career that fulfills her in a whole new way. She loves the
team she works with, enjoys their customers, and loves everything she's learning in the process. She'd never have guessed she would end up working in a
corporate setting on a computer all day, but nonetheless, this is ideal for her at
this time in her life.

Your Personal Growth

The fifth area I'd like you to contemplate is your personal growth. You may be wondering what this is. By my definition, this is you thinking about who you want to be and how you want to grow. Maybe there are skills you want to learn. Maybe there are qualities you want to acquire. Lou Holtz, a former NFL coach, once said, "You're either growing or you're dying." It's up to us. That's what this area of life is all about.

Bonnie used to get fearful whenever she contemplated change. Although she wanted to make some changes in her life, every time she took the first step, she got nervous, worried, and then couldn't sleep. While attending a women's retreat weekend I facilitated, she began working on approaching change in a different way. She learned how to think differently about change, and then she started with tiny changes in her life. She learned several calming activities that worked well for her: reading, classical music, yoga, talking to her girlfriend, saying a rosary prayer, and going to her favorite lake nearby. So, whenever she began to get scared, she would engage in one or several of these activities.

Eventually, Bonnie was able to approach bigger and bigger changes. She left her career to start her own business. As you can imagine, the unpredictability of this was high. But through her private coaching, she kept growing her courage muscles, and through her professional training, she learned the technical skills needed to be a successful entrepreneur.

Another client of mine, Tracy, retired and did not know what to do with herself anymore. She had attached a lot of her self-esteem to the children she'd taught for thirty years. She also felt bored and lonely with so much time on her hands. She knew she needed to grow by learning to create a new life and routine for herself.

To assist her with this, I had Tracy sign up for my Living Your Passions ~ Finding Your Purpose Coaching Program. She was able to identify what she was most passionate about and how to incorporate those passions into her daily life. Through the program, Tracy realized how important it was for her to keep children in her life, how much she wanted to learn how to paint, how badly she wanted to travel to national parks, how much she wanted to study ancestry, and how important living a healthy lifestyle was to her. All of these desires became areas of personal growth and development for her. Together, we mapped out plans to honor every passion in her life, and soon, her self-esteem skyrocketed. With an exciting and focused new agenda, she was no longer bored or lonely. Her life became one of meaning, joy, and stimulation.

(If you'd like more detailed information about this short-term coaching program, visit: *cindydwhitmer.com/livingyourpassion.*)

What the Wise King Knows

Getting crystal clear about everything you want in your life is a critically important part of your mid-life makeover. You cannot get what you don't know you want. Make it a priority to specifically identify what you would like your life to look like in the areas of health, relationships, finances, professional life, and personal growth. If ideas come up for you that are outside of these five areas, spend time identifying those as well. The clearer the picture you create, the better your results will be.

Remember not to limit yourself with this vision. You do not have to understand all the details of how these things can be created in your life. You do not have to know every step of the process to incorporate everything. Right now, all you need to know is what you want. Period. Wondering whether you can make your desires a reality is just a negative distraction. Just being able to name what you want, write it down, and read it out loud or tell someone you trust is a terrific start.

Like Martin Luther King Jr. famously said, "You do not have to see the whole staircase to take the first step." This step in your makeover is all about knowing what you want your life to look and feel like in every area. When I coach my clients through this step, I also teach them the power of writing specific affirmations related to their desires and how reading them regularly while visualizing them will create quicker results. For now, just remember that loving yourself fully and living on your terms is the ultimate goal. The desired result of your makeover is to make these middle years the best of your life so far. Imagine what would get you there! That's all you need to do.

Key Takeaways

- Knowing what you want, need, and desire in all areas of your life is critical to your happiness.

- You cannot get what you want if you don't know what that is.
- Creating your own definition of what it means to be holistically healthy is paramount.
- The nature of your relationships strongly affects the quality of your life.
- How you manage your finances is parallel to how you manage other areas of your life.
- Your unique professional expression must be meaningful and satisfying.
- Identifying and incorporating your passions into your daily life will sky-rocket your self-esteem.
- You don't have to know the details of how to incorporate what you want right now.

Now It's Your Turn: Off to the Cinema—Your Biopic

Imagine you're sitting in a movie theater watching a biographical film based on your ideal life right now. You are the star. In each scene, you see yourself living out your ideal life in all the key areas you've read about in this chapter: health, relationships, finances, professional life, and personal growth. Notice how much you love yourself, how wonderful you feel, and how satisfying your life looks to you. Take note of everything you do, where you are, who you're with, and how you live out your daily life. See all of this in grand detail and soak up the satisfaction you feel from loving yourself unapologetically and living on your terms. Make this the best movie you'll ever see and the greatest performance of your life—Oscar-worthy, of course.

Coming Up Next . . .

Now that you've identified what you want in five key areas of your life, we are going to move on to the next step of your makeover, which is all about eliminating energy drainers. By clarifying what you do want, you now know more about what you do *not* want. So, the time has come to begin to get rid of everything you no longer want, need, or use. We'll also look at your messes and tolerations—which are things left undone, broken, or bogging you down in some other way—and make plans to bring those issues to completion.

Chapter Six

Eliminating Energy Drainers

WHEN KAREN WAS IN HER FIFTIES SHE FOUND HERSELF AT A CROSSROADS. HER three adult sons were still living with her, her house felt like a zoo, and the stress was beginning to take its toll. Karen felt her life was out of her control. Her sons did not pick up after themselves and expected her to continue to make dinner every night after she had worked all day at the office, just as she had their entire lives. None of them carried any financial responsibility for the food, utilities, or property, let alone the chores involved in keeping up a home. Even their laundry would consume the laundry room until she begged them to take care of it.

Karen was tired, drained, and felt taken for granted. She loved her sons so much and feared that if she started asking anything of them, they would be angry. She believed she would miss them if they moved out, but she also longed for the space to be her own.

When Karen and I began working through The Mid-Life Makeover Method, she woke up to how she had created and was perpetuating this pattern with her kids. She was continuing to be the full-time mother she'd been since they were born, providing for their every need and not expecting them to do anything in return. Therefore, she wasn't allowing them to grow up.

Then, she got crystal clear about what she wanted her life to look like. She wanted her sons in her life, but she really wanted to live alone. At this stage in her life, she really only wanted to be responsible for herself. She wanted to eat popcorn for dinner sometimes or not have to have dinner at all. She wanted peace and quiet in her home and for it to stay clean and orderly without a lot of necessary upkeep. She wanted to turn one of the bedrooms into an exercise room and the other into a craft room for her scrapbooking hobby. This was not currently possible with all of her young-adult sons living there.

Once Karen knew what she really wanted, she began to easily identify what she did *not* want. Knowing what you do want helps you understand what you do not want. Anything we no longer want, need, or use is an energy drainer. In Karen's example, all three of her young-adult sons, as well as all of their material possessions, were energy drainers as long as they were still in her house.

Her feelings of obligation to provide dinner every night and a roof over their heads without any financial responsibility was another type of energy drainer. Sometimes, circumstances we put up with fall into the category of an energy drainer as well. Other types of tolerations would be anything broken (like a lightbulb that needs replacing); anything being neglected that needs attention (like a toothache); clutter anywhere (the attic, the basement, the living room); or even an imbalance in relationships, such as Karen and her sons. She was over-giving, and they were under-functioning.

Eventually, through our coaching together, Karen was able to transition with her sons. They each set a goal date for moving out and also shared responsibilities for the bills and chores while still living there. She was able to have heart-to-heart conversations with them about her desire to live on her own and change the purpose of several rooms in her home to facilitate her current lifestyle. Although completing the transition took time, everyone felt better about the living arrangements, which were based on greater equity and respect for everyone.

I'm thrilled to tell you that Karen lives by herself now and is totally loving it! Her home is set up just as she wants it, with every room filling a specific purpose, keeping her passions easily accessible and her routines honored. She loves coming home from work now and nestling into her craft room to do a project or into her favorite chair to curl up and read. Maybe she makes dinner. Maybe she doesn't. Her choice. She doesn't have to think about anybody else for a change.

The weight that lifted off of her shoulders was tremendous because she was no longer denying herself the lifestyle she was ready for. Her life is simpler, quieter, and, quite frankly, more fun. She is enjoying the good company of herself. And the great news is that every one of her sons is now thriving on his own. Each of them has found a new place to live and has learned how to pay his bills and take care of his own lifestyle. Once a week, they all get together for dinner with Karen. They catch up and delight in their time together. (And for the record, sometimes Karen cooks for them because she wants to, sometimes they all go out to eat, and sometimes the guys bring food over for her!)

What Karen's example reminds us is that when we love ourselves fully and live on our terms, we can be happier than ever and make this the best time of our life! And everyone else benefits as well! The ripple effect in Karen's family included her sons feeling empowered to function on their own and create lives they truly wanted, without anything holding them back.

Let's take a look at six common types of energy drainers, so you can start to free yourself just like Karen did.

Energy Drainer #1: Clutter

Clutter is material items that are piled, scattered, or untidily present in a physical environment. Clutter may also be an excessive amount of stuff crowded into a place too small to properly accommodate it. Clutter could also be having more than one of a certain type of item even though only one can be utilized at a time. For example, you keep buying a white long-sleeved button-down shirt because you don't realize you have three other ones hanging in your closet with the tags still on them.

In The Mid-Life Makeover Method, I teach that clutter can also be anything you no longer want, need, or use, but that you keep around anyway. For example, I still have my wedding dress. You know, the one from 1990. My daughter doesn't want it. I obviously don't plan on wearing it again. Why do I still have it? Sentiment? Memories? Memorabilia and sentimental clutter are two of the biggest culprits in this category. Kaye, a radio show host who once interviewed me about simplifying our lives, admitted she had a rocking chair of her great-grandmother's and a letterman jacket of her father's, neither of which she used, but she just didn't know what to do with them. This is a common issue. We can't imagine throwing such things away and feel guilty about giving them away or selling them. Shouldn't we treasure these family heirlooms and just keep passing them down from one generation to the next?

This is one way clutter develops. Whether it's grandma's quilts; grandpa's tools; the outfit you wore coming home from the hospital when you were born; school projects; photo albums from the eighties; postcards from every vacation you've taken for the last thirty years; or the T-shirts, coffee mugs, caps, magnets, and other classic mementos you picked up along the way, all of these things are basically worthless. But they take up space on your shelves; in your closets; and in plastic tubs in your garage, basement, and attic—or, for about 10 percent of Americans, the storage sheds you rent because not everything you've acquired fits into your home.[1]

Clutter becomes an energy drainer. Every time you have to see it, step over it, think about it, move it, clean it, or go through it again because you've forgotten what's even there, it takes up space in your environment and in your mind. This is stressful at best. You feel overwhelmed and don't have the time or capacity to do anything about it. Draining. Very draining.

Energy Drainer #2: Disorganization

Much like clutter, disorganization is the lack of orderliness in your life. If you or your things are disorganized, you probably can't find anything easily. You may waste a lot of time searching for things and wondering where they are. This is frustrating for you. You may forget you even own something (like the shirt mentioned before) and end up wasting money to fill a need that you have already filled but have lost track of.

You can also be very disorganized with money and paying bills. You may not keep solid records of your spending and saving and end up getting yourself into some trouble, like not paying your bills on time and then being slapped with nasty late fees, which just consume you financially even more. You may be paying for services you don't utilize or for warranties you don't need. Many of the women I have worked with don't even know what credit cards they have, let alone the balances or interest rates.

Another key area of disorganization in women's lives is time. Many of my clients have struggled to organize their time well and find their balance. Because they have been over-giving, they run around in circles, trying to please everyone and everything they have said yes to, and end up meeting themselves coming and going. Do you think they're drained? Believe me, they are. Can you relate to this?

---

[1] Alexander Harris, "U.S. Self-Storage Industry Statistics," SpareFoot, January 27, 2021, *https://www.sparefoot.com/self-storage/news/1432-self-storage-industry-statistics/*.

Energy Drainer #3: Incompletes

Remember the lightbulb that needs to be replaced? That's an incomplete. Anything in your environment that's broken, malfunctioning, or left unfinished is an incomplete. The door that squeaks every time you open it, the weird clunking sound your car makes every time you start it, the dripping faucet in the kitchen—all incompletes.

Projects hanging over your head are also incompletes. The blanket you're still trying to finish sewing for the new grandbaby, the trim around the window in your bedroom you still intend to paint, the article for work you still need to collect appropriate research for, the seeds you have yet to plant in your garden, and the card you keep meaning to send are all incompletes.

Incompletes, no matter how big or small they seem, also take up energy and space in your mind, body, and environment. Every time you become aware of them *again*, you feel bad, anxious, concerned, guilty, out of control, frustrated, or inadequate.

This slowly chips away at your self-esteem and confidence. You get overwhelmed and embarrassed. This is why some people never invite friends over to their houses. This is why other people never allow themselves to have fun or treat themselves to something they really want. They're consumed with negativity and guilt about how their lives got out of control. They feel stuck.

Energy Drainer #4: Tolerations

Of course, every type of energy drainer I've mentioned so far could also fit into the category of a toleration because you're "tolerating" something—the broken toaster, the files stacked on your desk, the contents of your deceased mother's estate, and so on. However, here I'm referring to tolerations in your relationships. What I find in my coaching business is that nothing drains a woman more than dissatisfaction in a relationship.

As women, we are hardwired to value our relationships highly. Many women define themselves by the quality of their relationships and the roles they play in those relationships. So when there's discord, imbalance, conflict, or stress, women can suffer tremendously. One response they may have to this pain is tolerating behavior in others that is otherwise unacceptable. Therefore, it is draining.

An example would be Karen, who let her adult sons live rent-free and responsibility-free in her home well into their twenties. Another type of relationship toleration might be the friend who immediately calls you if she needs something and expects you to jump to it but is rarely there for you when you need a hand. Another one might be the family member who is consistently late for holiday dinners, cluelessly and carelessly holding up the festivities for everyone else. Another might be the partner you live with who calls you names, throws things, or even hits you. Another could be the boss who dumps extra work in your lap while letting your coworker slack off. Another may be your own choice to work yourself to exhaustion to take care of your elderly parents, so they don't have to go to a nursing home.

In short, what I teach in The Mid-Life Makeover Method is that tolerations are unhealthy, toxic dynamics in relationships that you allow to continue. You may do this out of love for others, out of fear of losing people, or because you think you just have to put up with it for some reason. No matter what your reasons are for putting up with these tolerations, they will drain you physically and emotionally. They will compromise your self-esteem and chip away at your confidence.

Energy Drainer #5: Beliefs

Sometimes, even our belief systems become drainers. For example, many of the women I work with grew up believing they weren't good enough, and they still hold that belief today. Others believe their sole purpose is to take care of other people. Many believe being abused is just the way life is. Some women believe you cannot divorce someone for any reason. Still others believe the God they grew up worshipping will punish them if they do anything wrong. Many were raised to believe you have to work extremely hard to make any money. Society's messages or cultural norms led some to believe women are to be subservient to men and are only capable of certain roles or careers.

Belief systems tend to develop very early in our lives. Sometimes, we developed them by being told them or learning about them in classes. Other times, we learned just by observation—living in our homes, watching our families function, experiencing life in our neighborhoods and communities, or watching certain media.

Then, when we grow up and it's time to live our lives on our own, these beliefs sometimes align with who we are and what we want, and sometimes they're a direct barrier to what we value and want to create. A belief becomes a drainer when it keeps you from living how you wish to live. A draining belief holds you back in some way and brings up feelings of depression or suffering when you think about it. When a belief you've had no longer aligns with who you authentically are, it's a drainer, and it needs to go.

In generation after generation of Kelly's family, the women were wives and stay-at-home mothers, while the men were husbands, fathers, and primary breadwinners. Everyone's roles were clear, and Kelly grew up witnessing this pattern play out day after day, year after year. From her standpoint, the men and women all seemed quite content in their roles and family life appeared balanced. This arrangement seemed to work well for everyone. Kelly had a happy, healthy childhood while being raised in this structure and environment.

However, as she grew up and contemplated her adult life, she realized she had no desire to get married or have children. Her dreams were different. She wanted to go to college, work in the corporate world, and travel extensively. She wanted to devote her time, money, and energy to exciting adventures. She wanted to live minimally and not be tied down to dependents or a serious commitment. Kelly had to eliminate the belief systems she grew up with in order to allow herself to live how she desired to live. Fortunately, she did, and even though her family was shocked and never really understood her "peculiar lifestyle," Kelly loved herself enough to live her way.

Energy Drainer #6: Habits

Much like our belief systems, habits can be learned early on by watching the people around us. If you watched your parents squander their money, you may find yourself doing the same as an adult. If you witnessed your teachers, coaches, or family members yelling when they wanted to get someone's attention, then you're likely to do that too.

We aren't doomed to act like other people, but we did learn a lot through observation when we were young and thought adults were showing us how to be adults! Therefore, we follow their lead. Sometimes that's a very positive thing; other times, it's a destructive pattern that needs to be broken.

Most women I work with can assess what habits in their lives are working for them well and which ones are draining them with very little thought.

Talia smoked for decades but knew she only did it out of habit, especially when she was emotionally upset about something or super tired from stress at work. She knew she wasn't addicted to nicotine, but rather had developed the habit of reaching for a cigarette when overly upset or stressed. Once she understood this was her pattern, she used our coaching and The Mid-Life Makeover Method to help her create other, healthier options when stressed or upset. After six months of gradually reducing her reliance on cigarettes, Talia was smoke-free, had more energy, saved the money she had been spending on cigarettes for a trip she'd always wanted to take, and was much happier in general. She was no longer drained by the habit.

Other draining habits my clients have overcome include numbing themselves with alcohol, excessive shopping, overworking, overeating, staying up until the middle of the night before sleeping, avoiding their feelings, neglecting their relationships, wasting their money, yelling, swearing, being late, driving too fast, gambling excessively, sexual promiscuity, and saying "yes" to things when they mean "no."

Take Off the Bricks

As you can see, there are many types of drainers in your life. Again, what makes them drainers is that they all cause stress of one kind or another, take up space in your environment or your mind, can cause overwhelm, or keep you stuck. A more spiritual perspective around drainers is that the more drainers you have in your life, the less space will be available to bring in the "new," which may mean new material things, new relationships, new ideas, or new opportunities. When you're consumed by drainers, you cannot open yourself up to more.

According to Coach University, when people first become aware of what drainers are, they discover they have between thirty and sixty of them.[2] No matter how many you currently have, imagine each one as a brick stacked on your shoulders. The more you have, the more difficult it is to balance yourself and your life and the more weighed down you become.

2   Coach U Inc., *Coach U's Essential Coaching Tools: Your Complete Practice Resource* (Hoboken: John Wiley & Sons, 2005).

This is why eliminating energy drainers is an important step in The Mid-Life Makeover Method. You've identified what you do want in your life, and now you can more clearly see what you do not want or what is no longer working well for you. When you become willing to let go of those things, you'll open the door and the space in your mind, your time, and your environment for what you truly want to come in.

Three Steps to Eliminate a Drainer

In The Mid-Life Makeover Method, you follow a three-step process for eliminating the drainers you've discovered.

Step One: Prioritize

There are several ways to prioritize your list of drainers. You can categorize them from the easiest to the hardest to eliminate. You can categorize them from the most disruptive drainer to the least disruptive drainer. Or you can arrange them from which ones you have the least control over to the ones you have the most control over.

For example, an "easy" drainer to eliminate might be the thank-you notes you have yet to write for the birthday gifts you received, whereas a "hard" drainer to eliminate might be cleaning out your garage. A very disruptive drainer might be your car that's not running at all, causing you to have to find alternative transportation on a regular basis, whereas a slightly disruptive one may be the overflowing trash in your kitchen. A drainer you have full control over may be your unorganized office file cabinet, and a drainer you do not have full control over may be the outdated will you and your spouse have yet to update together.

Mapping out your drainers this way can help you put a timely plan in place for eliminating them that gets your momentum going and allows you to experience some quick successes, which is energizing and encourages you to keep going.

Step Two: Decide Where to Begin

In *The Success Principles*™, author Jack Canfield teaches us the four Ds for starting to eliminate drainers. The four Ds are do, delegate, delay, and dump. In other words, do it yourself, delegate it to someone else, delay it for a later time, or dump the idea altogether.[3]

Whatever approach you take for each drainer, you want to indicate on your list who will be handling the drainer and set a completion date. Create a manageable timeline for each drainer based on the enormity or simplicity of the job and how few or how many people are required to get organized and work together to take care of it.

Remember, if you're delegating, you may need to empower coworkers, family members, or whoever is involved to get excited about taking care of this drainer. Also, you may want to hire experts to help with some of your drainers. Be willing to spend money to take care of your drainers when appropriate. Maybe you've been meaning to landscape your yard for the past two years and just haven't gotten to it. You may have the skills and equipment to do it yourself, but you've never found the proper time to follow through. Perhaps you've learned it's best to hire a landscaping company for this task. That's perfectly acceptable, and you'll still feel the relief of having it done even without doing it yourself. And actually, you may feel relieved at the point of hire, even before the job is completely done! With people assigned to the drainers and goal dates set, you can begin to eliminate them.

Some drainers may have felt important at one point but no longer do at this time. I recently let go of an idea I had to redo our dining room. I felt it was outdated, and I wanted to replace the furniture and curtains. This was on my mind for some time. Yet, I wasn't taking any action to complete it. I also thought it best to sell our piano because no one was playing it regularly. Yet, I hadn't done anything about it. Then I realized I liked having the piano as a decoration and to play once in a while. Because I hadn't taken action on either in a long time, I decided to just dump the ideas. Obviously—at this time, anyway—neither was important to me and, therefore, the ideas weren't draining me anymore.

Step Three: Reward Yourself

Reward yourself for the completion of every drainer as you go along. Start by checking them off your list every time you finish one. That's a reward in itself.

---

3   Jack Canfield, *The Success Principles™: How to Get from Where You Are to Where You Want to Be* (New York: Harper Collins, 2007), 201.

Another reward would be to allow yourself to participate in an energy-producing activity of your choice. This could be anything you truly love to do, find relaxing, or are passionate about. If you love to go horseback riding, you could set up riding time for the week after you get the garage cleaned out.

If you eliminate drainers as a family, you might plan a special outing everyone would enjoy after eliminating your top ten drainers or after your first thirty days of eliminating drainers. Whatever will encourage everyone and energize everyone to keep going is what you want to promise as an incentive.

Celebrate every success in some way that fits your budget and time. Crossing them off your list, patting yourself on the back, ordering takeout the night you finish, buying yourself something you've been wanting, or doing anything meaningful to you are all valid ways to reward yourself.

Intangible rewards will automatically happen as well. For example, when the women I coach eliminate their drainers, they just feel better and lighter. They tend to be calmer and happier people. They find it liberating to eliminate the drainers and feel empowered by the process. Their confidence levels rise, their attitudes shift in a positive direction, and they feel more grateful. All these emotions offset the overwhelm, stress, depression, and frustration they felt before. Your time will also be freed up with less on your to-do list hanging over your head. You'll have more open space in your schedule, environment, mind, and heart for anything new that may be trying to get in.

Life will be simpler for sure. The relationships that were draining you will take less time and energy from you as well. You will have put up strong boundaries, had tough conversations, and learned how to take things less personally. You will focus your energy on the more positive people in your life and on having more fun.

You will have sorted through your old, destructive beliefs and adopted new ones that serve you much better. The same is true of your old habits; you will have let go of the old and found the new. (We'll cover both of these topics in greater detail in later chapters.)

Eliminating energy drainers means letting go of the old and letting go of what you no longer want, need, or use anymore—from material things to beliefs and habits. Drainers also include anything incomplete in your life like unresolved relationship issues or unfinished projects. Everything that drains you is part of your "old story," and eliminating them to bring in the new is part of your "new story." You've woken up, gotten clear about what you want, and gotten rid of everything you no longer need. Your mid-life makeover is well underway!

Key Takeaways

- Energy drainers sap your energy physically and emotionally.
- Drainers come in many forms—from clutter to disorganization to incompletes to beliefs and habits.
- Relationships can even be energy drainers.
- You can eliminate most drainers through a three-step process: prioritize, decide where to begin, and reward yourself.
- Drainers can be done yourself, delegated to others, delayed for later, or dumped.
- Creating a goal completion time for each drainer helps set yourself up for success.
- Tangible rewards can be planned for every time you complete a drainer.
- Intangible rewards will come with every completion as well.

Now It's Your Turn: Your Personal Tour

Get out a notepad or anything you can make a long list on and take a lengthy tour through all of your environments, identifying any energy drainer you notice or feel. Walk through every room and physical space of any of your properties or workplaces. Think about unfinished tasks personally and professionally. Consider your relationships and what needs to change. Look over your financial picture for anything out of place for you. Do a quick assessment of your emotional and physical health. Examine your beliefs. Recognize your habits. Check every corner of your world and write down anything and everything that's causing you distress in any way. This is your list of drainers. Then, take the time to prioritize them using the options described above that best fit you. Next, make specific plans and completion dates for the ones you want to start with. Reward yourself every time you eliminate a drainer.

Coming Up Next . . .

Now that you've done a personal tour of your outer world, we are going to address your inner world in the next chapter. Your mind can be your worst enemy or your best friend. Mastering your mindset is within your power and will lead you to the life you've always wanted. If I could only teach you one step of The Mid-Life Makeover Method, this would be the one. Get excited! Your makeover is about to get even more dramatic!

Chapter Seven
Mastering Your Mindset

Darla worked in education for decades. She was very comfortable in the teaching role she held in the school system. She was confident, secure, and well-liked. Late in her career, Darla decided it was time to pursue a new role. She became an administrator. This was a bigger change than she could have ever imagined. Her relationships with the students, the staff, and the parents all shifted. Even though she was told there was a learning curve with the position that took most people months to grasp, Darla was nervous every time she didn't know the answer to a question or how to carry out a specific task. Her inner monologue sounded like this: *I don't know if I can do it. I feel like I'm fresh out of college, even though I'm not. They're going to lose patience with me. The stress is going to take over my life. I used to think I was smart. I hope I haven't made a big mistake!*

Every day on her commute to and from school, she found her thoughts heading in this direction. Negative and based on fear, her thoughts were starting to consume her. Thinking this way set the tone for a challenging day, at best. This left her less equipped to be calm, take her time, and handle her new agenda with patience and ease. Instead, she would get even more stressed-out and afraid she was going to fail. Ending the day by driving home with these thoughts added to her discomfort, which led to evenings at home spent worried, anxious, and dreading the next day. She wasn't sleeping well, and she was emotionally unavailable to her spouse.

So when she approached me about coaching her, I knew mastering her mindset was going to be a significant piece of her mid-life makeover. I wanted her to learn how her thoughts could change her life. We dove into The Mid-Life Makeover Method, and she quickly began to understand how her mind could be her best friend or her enemy.

We examined her self-talk, identifying specific messages that were running through her mind on a regular basis, practiced catching those thoughts, and reframed them. When she said things like, "I'm afraid I'm going to fail," I had her write down a new thought that countered that one. Mastering your mindset includes choosing new ways to think about a situation and framing the new thoughts to represent what you *want* to create. An example of Darla's would be, *I am learning more and more every day. I am willing to believe I am perfect for this position and am getting more confident in my new role all the time.*

It's not about lying to yourself about what isn't yet true. It's about laying the groundwork in your mind for what you want to manifest. Darla wanted to feel secure and confident in her role as the principal of her school. She wanted to show up well for the students, staff, and parents, and be able to go home every day feeling good about the impact she'd had. We can use our thoughts to lead us to the realization of what we want.

In under three months of working on her mindset, Darla was able to look forward to work every day and be productive and happier in her role. She found herself driving home feeling more satisfied with her experiences and peaceful about what she had yet to learn. Her anxiety levels dropped dramatically, long before she knew how to carry out every task her job required. This led to evenings of relaxation and delight with her spouse that weren't consumed with how the day had gone or what tomorrow would look like.

This is what a healthy mindset can do for anyone. Internationally renowned author Wayne Dyer taught that people average between fifty thousand and sixty thousand thoughts per day.[4] He indicated that we repeat 95 percent of those thoughts day after day. In other words, our inner dialogue is as habitual and routine as eating breakfast or brushing our teeth. He also taught that what we focus on expands. So, if I suggest you think about elephants, you're going to immediately think about elephants and will likely see a picture of one in your mind related to some previous experience you've had with one. Having planted that seed in your mind, you may find yourself stumbling upon pictures, stories, toys, or any number of other elephant-related products. The mind is that powerful.

4   Wayne W. Dyer, *Change Your Thoughts, Change Your Life: Living the Wisdom of the Tao* (London: Hay House, 2007).

Because we have so many thoughts every day and what we focus on gets bigger, it's very important to be aware of what dialogue is happening in our minds. All of us have at least two voices in our heads: positive self-talk and negative self-talk.

Positive vs. Negative Self-Talk

Positive self-talk is the encouraging, empowering, optimistic messages you give yourself in your mind or out loud. When you say things like "I can do it!" or "I love myself!" you're engaging in positive self-talk. With this healthy mindset, you're far more likely to move through your days with joy and confidence. On the other hand, if you say things like "I'm not good enough" or "I'm a disaster at relationships," you're going down a spiral of negative self-talk and will likely become discouraged, depressed, or overwhelmed.

When you speak kindly to yourself, you're better able to face any challenge or delight in any activity of the day. You'll smile more, be kinder to people on your path, and be able to concentrate on what's most important to you.

However, when you speak negatively toward yourself, you're setting yourself up to be miserable and ill-equipped to accomplish what you have in mind for the day without experiencing significant struggle, pressure, or stress in the process. You won't show up in your relationships the way you would prefer to, and then you'll end up feeling even worse about yourself. Thus, your negative dialogue will disintegrate even further.

Limiting Beliefs

So, where does the negative voice come from? And how come some people have more positive self-talk than others? The voices in our heads begin developing very early in our lives. As children, we took in the experiences of the people around us. Our most significant players likely had the most impact on the beliefs we developed.

If you were mostly surrounded by emotionally healthy, happy, reliable adults, you probably heard them using a lot of positive self-talk. You probably heard them share an optimistic view of life, the world, and other people. They probably spoke to you with a lot of encouragement and joy. You took this in and, from these experiences, developed a set of beliefs that matched theirs.

You probably viewed people, life, and the world as a safe, loving, fun, and nurturing place. You probably thought you were a "nice girl" or that you could do anything. Because you were raised with this as your primary experience, you carried that right into adulthood and created more positive experiences. The dialogue in your head stayed consistent with that healthy upbringing.

Many of the women I work with had the opposite upbringing. Perhaps their families were riddled with stress, anger, abuse, or some other form of conflict. Often, their parents weren't parented in a healthy way, so they were ill-equipped to provide a positive, encouraging atmosphere for their children. The emotional wounds they never healed began to surface in their parenting, which led to inconsistencies, chaos, criticism, abuse, neglect, or other kinds of toxicity. The key players in your life may have struggled a lot in their lives and formed the view that life is hard, the world isn't fair, or people can't be counted on. Then, because they've had many negative experiences themselves, their inner dialogue was negative, which showed up in the parenting and the role-modeling they provided.

With this type of experience, you're likely to feel anxious, worried, unsafe, or fearful. You may question whether you can trust people, or you may believe that your life is going to go a certain way no matter what you do. The powerlessness you feel and the critical nature of those around you causes you to develop beliefs like, *I am not good enough. Nothing goes well for me or my family. No one in my life is happy.* These repetitive, negative, defeating kinds of statements are what are called limiting beliefs.

Limiting beliefs are just that. They are beliefs you've adopted that represent a limited view of yourself, life, people, opportunities, or the world. With this type of belief, you'll hold yourself back (limit yourself) from really dreaming or going for anything that has, in your mind, been out of reach. It will be difficult to see beyond what you've experienced thus far, and you're likely to think good things only happen to other people or that you're stuck. You'll feel like a victim in your own life and won't be able to see all the possibilities before you.

With limiting beliefs comes a negative voice and an unhappy life. Limiting beliefs are articulated in the form of negativity toward yourself, others, and the world. Because what you focus on expands, proof of the negativity and limiting beliefs shows up in tangible ways in your life, which further confirms your reality to you. Therefore, you become stuck in a cycle of negativity and a life of limitations.

Gay Hendricks, author of *The Big Leap*, teaches what he calls the "Upper Limit Problem." He says that along with the limiting beliefs we carry with us from our earliest experiences comes a limit to the amount of good we will allow into our lives. This "good" could be related to health, material abundance, love, joy, professional success, or anything else we might consider wonderful. When we reach our upper limit (which is different for everyone), we'll likely get uncomfortable and sabotage ourselves in some way, interrupting the flow of positive results and experiences in our lives.[5]

With The Mid-Life Makeover Method, I show women how to begin to turn this cycle in a positive direction. First, I help my clients recognize their negative beliefs (which they may or may not have been conscious of previously) and catch when those beliefs are operating. Next, I help them to see the effects of believing as they do. Then we begin to rewrite the belief system to support what they want to create in their lives. With practice, they begin to turn things around, eventually rewiring their brains with a whole new track that leads to more positive results in their lives. Then, they can break the glass ceiling of their upper limit and allow more good to come into their experiences.

The T.F.A. Cycle

Beyond just knowing your limiting beliefs and the self-talk you're using, it's also important to understand the fallout from them. To illustrate this, I created what I call the "T.F.A. Cycle." This stands for the thoughts, feelings, and actions cycle. Let me explain.

First, you have a thought. (Remember, beliefs are just thoughts you keep thinking.) Then, what you think creates a feeling inside of you. Based on how you feel, you then choose some type of action. So, our thoughts lead to our feelings, which lead to our actions. Our actions will then lead to another thought, which creates another feeling, which leads to more action. It's a cycle, and our lives are made up of a series of these cycles. We go around and around and around, feeling like a hamster on a wheel and doing the same thing over and over again, satisfied or not.

5   Gay Hendricks, *The Big Leap: Conquer Your Hidden Fear and Take Life to the Next Level* (New York: Harper One, 2009), 1.

Let's say you're walking on the sidewalk downtown and you notice a homeless person sitting on the corner with a sign that reads, "Anything would help." You think, *Hm, I bet that's a drug addict. I bet she's lazy.* Then you probably feel judgmental, disgusted, or annoyed. You'll likely change your route, avoid the person, or walk around them, ignoring them or maybe even giving them a dirty look. Your next thought as you go on with your day might be, *This world is such a mess.* (And the cycle continues.)

Or maybe, when you saw the homeless person, you thought, *Oh my gosh, I wonder what happened in her life that she finds herself sitting here begging for help? I feel sorry for her.* Then you probably feel compassion, generosity, or kindness. You likely get out your wallet, grab some money, and walk right up to her and give it to her, maybe even with a smile or a hug. Your next thought as you go on with your day might be, *I am so grateful for my life!* (And the cycle continues.)

What if you want to make a change in your life? Let's say you feel fat, and you're trying to lose weight. You start with a well-intentioned weight loss journey. This is what a negative T.F.A. Cycle would be like:

Thoughts = *I have tried everything already, and nothing has worked. I can't do this.*

Feelings = Defeated, depressed, and hopeless

Actions = Emotionally overeating, remaining a couch potato, and resigning to staying fat

This is what a positive T.F.A. Cycle would be like:

Thoughts = *I can do this. I've overcome other challenges in my life. I'm worth it!*

Feelings = Motivated, inspired, excited, and hopeful

Actions = Trying new recipes, daily exercise, and joining a weight loss support group

Knowing your patterns of thought and understanding the feelings and actions they lead you to is a critical piece of your makeover. If you're not getting the results you want in any area of your life, check your thoughts first. Listen to the voices in your head and the self-talk you're using. These are your biggest clues to how you've gotten where you are today. When your life is working well for you, you'll find a pattern of positive self-talk, empowering thoughts, healthy feelings, and inspired actions. When your life isn't working well for you, you'll find a pattern of negative self-talk, debilitating thoughts, destructive feelings, and actions that don't serve your greater goals.

As you begin to master your mindset, changing your thoughts to change your life, you'll think differently, feel better, and take actions that align with who you authentically are and what you really want. However, this isn't like a college degree, where once you have it, you always have it. Mastering your mindset is a moment-to-moment lifestyle. You can be thinking in healthy ways one moment and start down a completely different path the next moment. This is common and simply needs to be noticed and turned around as quickly as possible.

Sometimes, you can go for days, weeks, or even months—secure in your new mindset, feeling fabulous, and getting consistently awesome results—and then, out of the blue, something can happen that throws you off completely. These are referred to as triggers.

Triggers

A trigger can be any kind of experience that causes you to have a strong emotional reaction. They can come in the form of a specific word used by someone, a memory, dream, nightmare, smell, sight, or sound—really anything that's tied to a previous emotional experience for you. Triggers may be tied to heartwarming, wonderful moments in your life that cause you to ooze with joy, love, and gratitude. Or they may be tied to drama, grief, trauma, stress, or other very challenging times in your life and bring on tremendous distress, anxiety, anger, depression, or other difficult emotions.

Have you ever had someone say something to you, quite innocently, and you suddenly felt crazy and bit their head off in anger? Now, you might just be that volatile, but more than likely, you were triggered. In some way, consciously or unconsciously, that experience was familiar, and you were responding not only to the moment but more so to the history that matched it. In the world of psychology, there's the phrase, "If it's hysterical, it's historical." In other words, if you're acting hysterical, it's probably due to your history. This is such powerful information.

Mastering Your Triggers

When you realize you're being triggered, you can take a deep breath and show compassion to yourself (and others around you). You can find the truth about what's bothering you by connecting the dots of "the now" with "the past."

Here's an example: When I was married, I felt my husband was very controlling. I believed he felt he was in charge of me and that I was supposed to do what he wanted at all times without question. This came in the form of what clothes I should wear, how I should do my hair, what I should think about something, whether or not to apply for a job, how I should be spending my time, etc.

Years (yes, *years*—keep that in mind) after my divorce, I developed a serious relationship with my current partner and moved in with him. Because I work from home, I'm there all day most days, and I can take care of little needs for the house from time to time. One day, my beloved told me to open the curtains in the upper-level room at a certain time and close the ones on the west side of the house at a certain time. He was giving me a specific schedule for all the curtains—telling me exactly what to do and when to do it. Was *he* trying to control me, too?

I love nature and natural sunlight. In my single life previously, I would have all the curtains open all day long and close them at dusk or dark. So, when he told me I should open these curtains and close these other curtains at a certain time, I thought, *Who do* you *think* you *are trying to tell* me *when I can have the curtains open or not? I live here too. I'm here all day. I'll do what I want.* (I was clearly triggered.)

Before I did a lot of personal growth work, I would have verbalized (with strong emotion) the thoughts I was having about this. I would have likely accused him of trying to control me and, in rebellion, not done a thing he had asked me to do. This likely would have taken us down an unpleasant, emotional road with hurt feelings all around and silence at the dinner table.

But because I had done my personal growth work, I was able to take his instructions and consider them rationally without my trigger-based thoughts taking center stage. I realized my beloved wasn't trying to control me by any stretch of the imagination. He was trying to control the temperature of the house and keep it regulated and comfortable in the most efficient way. He's an engineer, and this is one of his strengths. He's not the same person as my ex-husband, but because this situation appeared to be the same initially, I felt the same way I had in some of the experiences I'd had in my marriage. My history was trying to make me hysterical in the present moment by triggering me.

This is just one example of hundreds of kinds of triggers that can happen to you. Grief, especially, can bring many triggers. When you miss a loved one who has died, any time you see someone who dresses like them, see someone who drives a similar car to the one they did, or hear their favorite song on the radio, you can be triggered. When I lived in Iowa, we raked our fallen leaves into the street, and large trucks scooped them up and hauled them away. One day, two little boys were playing in the piles of leaves in the street, but the truck driver did not see them. Both boys were killed instantly. Every year when the leaves fall, the grief of those who loved the boys is triggered, and strong emotions surface. These feelings need to be honored and expressed in a healthy way. When that's done, life can resume. Generally, triggers cause temporary reactions.

An important piece of mastering your mindset when triggers come is examining the thoughts the trigger has created. For example, in my curtain situation, the thoughts tied to my history were, *He's trying to control me. He thinks I'm too dumb to know when to open and close curtains. No matter what I do, it's never enough. I'm just here to do what he says.*

Those are debilitating, painful thoughts. They cut very deep and are tied to all kinds of devastating experiences—dynamics with myself and in my relationships with men—and could easily chip away at my self-confidence and self-esteem if I bought into them again. Mastering your mindset means you don't buy into them and recognize that they aren't true or real in the present moment. They are triggers. They are from the past. They need to be healed.

Finding new thoughts that are true now (or could be true) will be very healing. Again, with the example of the curtains, what I really believe is *My beloved needs my help to regulate our home's temperature while he's away. He knows the best way to do this and wants to keep me comfortable and save us money on utilities. He loves me and cares for me and our home. He appreciates my help with this. We are a team.*

Notice how much healthier those thoughts sound and how much better they feel. They are the truth too. I often say to my clients in our coaching sessions, "What else could be true right now?" This is a great checkpoint for you when you're experiencing a trigger and you want to master your mindset so you can feel better and stay calm.

Fear

According to the dictionary, fear is "an unpleasant emotion caused by the belief that someone or something is dangerous, likely to cause pain, or a threat."[6] Notice the word "belief" is right there in the middle of the definition. This tells us that fear isn't necessarily reality-based, but it's generated by a belief about someone or something around you.

Author Jack Canfield says fear stands for "fantasized experiences appearing real."[7] Again, fears are not necessarily based on facts but are instead based on appearances or interpretations made up in our minds.

In both ways, fear is conjured up in our minds. Fear is created by us. Now, if a saber-toothed tiger appears in front of you, please run. If the plane is going down, please fasten your seat belt and hope for the best. If a tornado is in your view, take shelter immediately. Clearly, fear is appropriate and understandable in these scenarios.

Most of the time, however, fear is unnecessary and made up. Much like worry, we fear things that we have no control over or that are very, very unlikely to happen. Falling prey to our fears does nothing but cause us more undue stress.

Just like Darla, who started the new job and quickly convinced herself she would fail, you cannot function as well when feeling this way and bearing these thoughts. Fear can be paralyzing. Carrying it around with you will keep you from trying new things, asking for what you need, or being happy. Yet, it's all in your mind. Made up. Useless.

Let's say you're widowed and in your fifties. You miss having companionship and cannot imagine living the rest of your life alone. However, any time you think of dating, you feel fear. Your inner dialogue might be something like, *What if everyone out there is a liar? What if no one will even talk to me, let alone take me*

---

6   Lexico, s.v., "Fear," accessed April 23, 2022, *https://www.lexico.com/en/definition/fear*.
7   Canfield, *The Success Principles™*, 116.

out for a nice dinner? What if they think I'm stupid or ugly or uninteresting? What if I can't figure out how to set up a profile on an online dating site? It's all fear.

These fears are very common and understandable for mid-lifers. At the same time, if you truly desire to date so you can find companionship in life, you'll need to face your fears and go after what you want anyway. The truth is that if someone thinks you're uninteresting, unattractive, or whatever, you would be no worse off than before you started. You cannot lose what you do not have. But if you don't even try, you'll be guaranteed not to find companionship. Which is worse?

Dismantle Your Fears

My friend Dani wanted to ask her boss for a raise. She found her boss very intimidating but was tired of waiting to get paid what she felt she was worth. However, she was petrified. What if her boss didn't think she deserved it? What if her boss got angry with her for asking? What if all she got from the risk was a big "no" and embarrassment?

I asked her about the thoughts behind the fear so she could start dismantling them. She was fearful her boss wouldn't think she deserved it. And what if she didn't? Would that be the end of the world? All we are talking about here is a difference of opinion. It wouldn't have to be tragic, right? And why would the boss be angry with her just for asking? (What kind of person is this boss, anyway?) If the boss is an angry person, Dani is likely to have witnessed how that plays out at the office before. Therefore, there wouldn't be any big surprises in this case. And so what if the boss said, "No!" to her request? She wouldn't be out anything because she didn't have it in the first place. If she chose to be embarrassed about having asked, then there's more mindset work to be done.

Most fears are a waste of time. There are very few emergencies in life. Think through your fears and find the thoughts behind them so you can dismantle them. Dismantling them involves examining them more closely and challenging their validity. If you find something to be genuinely afraid of, then put safety systems in place with your overall wellness in mind. Otherwise, reframe your thoughts from a fantasized point of view to a reality-based point of view. Do this until you can find enough strength to move forward, despite the fear, with whatever you want to do.

Becoming 100 percent fearless isn't the goal—although that would be nice! Mastering your mindset around fear is about sorting through what you tell yourself that leads to the fear and finding new ways to think about it. Ultimately, you want to be able to feel more courage than fear by mastering your mindset so you can take inspired steps toward what you want and need, despite the fear and worry. Remember, many people on their dying day express regret for things they did not say or do in their lifetime. Don't set yourself up to be one of them.

Dismantling My Own Fears

Before I decided to divorce my husband, I had fears of my own to dismantle. One of my greatest fears was that our children would be devastated, and their lives would be ruined. They were such great kids, and I loved them so much. I felt like I had a really good relationship with both of them, and I didn't want to ruin that by divorcing their dad. The teenage years can be challenging enough on a good day, let alone with a major life disruption!

I also feared financial stress and struggle, as I knew my income would be drastically reduced by leaving the marriage. Even though I had a full-time job, I did not make nearly the amount of money my husband did, nor would I have benefits anymore. What would that mean for me financially, now and in the future?

I even feared the counseling center's (my workplace) reputation could be damaged by my personal decision. It was a nonprofit faith-based center in a conservative small town in Kansas that relied on donations to survive, and I was the executive director—the primary figure representing the agency. Being a divorcée may have been a bit too nontraditional or considered inappropriate. I thought I might also lose some credibility with my therapy clients. Would they think I couldn't help them with their lives if my own life was falling apart?

Part of my mid-life makeover required me to face my fears and dismantle them so I could get clear about what I most needed and wanted in my life moving forward. I did not want to base my life decisions on fear—that's a setup for disaster!

One of the ways to dismantle a fear is to look at your history for evidence that supports you in overcoming it. Regarding my children's lives being ruined, I thought of how my own life had turned out despite my parents' divorce when I was a teenager. Although it was a very troubling time for everyone in my family, we survived it. I could admit that some very positive things came out of that transition as well. Perhaps that could be true for my children. Also, the kids were teenagers, and I felt secure we had had a great relationship up to that point, so why would it suddenly and drastically change, even in the case of a divorce? That wasn't a rational fear; it was emotional. I realized I needed to trust them to trust that I had their backs and that we would be more than okay no matter what we went through together.

My financial fears were easy to dismantle as well when I examined my history and the history of others. I thought about all the single parents I knew who appeared to be making it work just fine. I thought about both of my sets of grandparents, who had worked hard their whole lives and who probably had a lot less money than I had at that point. I remembered how, when I finished college, I literally had five dollars left in my bank account despite working five jobs to get through my senior year. I had built wealth ever since and couldn't even imagine what would have to happen to end up in that situation ever again, so why worry? I looked at my life as a whole to assess "my worth and my assets," so to speak, which included not only monetary accounts but my portion of our property, my education, my training, my skill set, my willingness to work hard, my network, my personality, and my faith. I knew I could make it no matter what.

As for my clients and the counseling center, I discussed my concerns with my board president. He understood, but he also reassured me that my life was my own and people would need to deal with the decisions I made in my personal life. Divorce wasn't uncommon, and people, in general, were very kind and understanding. I had a great reputation in the community, and I knew I could remain the respectful, steady, solid, approachable, and likable person I had always been. I trusted that once the word got out to my clients, they would address any concerns they had with me in our sessions, which would give me the golden opportunity to model my humanness even more and help them to understand how my own trials in life actually made me a stronger therapist for them. If, on the other hand, everything went downhill and I lost my job, I knew I could get another one or finally start my own business, which I had wanted to do for years. Either way, life was going to be okay.

Because I was able to look at my fears from a different perspective, I could move forward with the divorce and get on with my life. You can do this as well, no matter what way your fears are holding you back. Think about another way to look at the fears you have and explore the evidence in your own life or in the lives of others that supports you moving forward anyway. Life gets far more interesting when we stop hesitating and start uncovering new ways of being. Again, being 100 percent fearless isn't necessarily the goal. The goal is to learn to use your mind to help you manage your fears differently, from another angle, so you can move forward despite them.

You're in Control

No makeover would be complete or truly move you to love yourself fully and live on your terms without mastering your mindset. To make this the best time of your life, you must be able to make your mind your best friend instead of your greatest enemy. How you speak to yourself, what you choose to believe, and what you do with your triggers and fears will all play a significant role in moving you closer to or further from the life you know you want. The best part of all of this is that it's all in your head, and you're in complete control of that!

Key Takeaways

- Your mind can be your best friend or your worst enemy—your choice!
- You have fifty thousand to sixty thousand thoughts per day, which means you have that many chances to direct your life in the direction you most want to go.
- Positive self-talk is the empowering, encouraging voice that supports you.
- Negative self-talk is the debilitating, critical voice that depresses and deflates you.
- Beliefs are thoughts you just keep thinking.
- Limiting beliefs develop early in your life and direct your experiences whether you know it or not.
- Everyone has an upper limit of good they will allow into their lives, and when we reach it, we'll sabotage ourselves until we know better.
- The T.F.A. Cycle is the equation for how your thoughts lead to your feelings, which lead to your actions. To change the cycle, you need to change your thoughts.

- Triggers are anything in life that create an emotional reaction for you and are based on historically difficult experiences.
- Recognizing triggers for what they are can help you give them less power in your life.
- Fears are based on beliefs that cause you to experience uncomfortable emotions and can be dismantled to help you move past them.

Now It's Your Turn: Rewriting Beliefs (Your T.F.A. Cycle)

As I previously stated, if I could only teach people one of the steps in my courses and coaching programs, it would be Mastering Your Mindset. Most of us aren't taught about our mindsets or how to master them. Most of us don't even realize how our thoughts can change our lives. Therefore, most women I work with need the deeper dive of one of my Mid-Life Makeover Coaching Programs to truly master their mindsets. To find out more about those, go to *www.cindydwhitmer.com/coaching*.

In the meantime, a great first step in mastering your mindset is to practice rewriting your beliefs by using the T.F.A. Cycle explained above. Identify up to ten thoughts or beliefs you catch yourself repeatedly thinking and map them out this way:

Thoughts =

Feelings =

Actions =

Then, imagine how you would like to feel and what action you would like to take instead. Next, find a thought or belief that would support you in creating that result. Rewrite the new T.F.A. Cycle starting with the new thought that you would need to feel better and that would lead to the inspired action you wish to take.

Coming Up Next . . .

With a stronger, healthier mindset, you can set yourself up for an even better makeover by developing success habits. You will soon hear about the importance of taking everything you've learned so far in your makeover and writing specific goals, identifying habits you need to release, and identifying habits you need to adopt while learning how to incorporate them into your daily routines to support your joy-filled, meaningful life.

Chapter Eight
Developing Success Habits

WHEN ALICE JOINED THE 90-DAY MID-LIFE MAKEOVER PRIVATE COACHING Program, she felt completely out of control. She was overworking for a company that barely acknowledged her contributions. She wasn't sleeping well, was overweight, and was riddled with anxiety. She had forgotten how to have fun a long time ago and spent most of her time outside of work alone. Living out of boxes since her divorce, her home didn't feel relaxing to her; instead, it was another area she needed to fix.

She knew she couldn't sustain this lifestyle much longer. Her habits were destructive in nearly every area of her life. She wasn't eating healthy food, grabbing fast food from a drive-through every day instead because she was always in such a rush to either get to work or finally go home, exhausted from another twelve- to fourteen-hour day. There was no time for relaxation, exercise, hobbies, friendships, dating, family, or anything, really. Even the upkeep of her home and yard was challenging. She was running on empty all the time, and the stress caused her to feel anxious, which led to sleepless nights. This meant she would start the next day unable to get up with the first alarm, pushing the snooze button several times before dragging herself out of bed, rushing to get out the door so she could work again until evening with few breaks and no decent nourishment.

She said, "I go from self-loathing to self-compassion. I know I need to find my balance and have more fun. I want to be healthy, but I never seem to be able to stay motivated for very long. I feel better any time I stick to a plan."

Her makeover took much longer than ninety days (as did my own) but was well worth her efforts. Her self-awareness grew as she became more and more honest with herself about how she had contributed to her life turning out the way it had. She got clearer about how she wanted her life to look in every area. She knew she wanted to continue working for the company, but she only wanted to work the forty hours required for her position and not give up any earned vacation anymore.

She knew she wanted to exercise regularly, eat more real food she prepared herself, and lose twenty pounds. She knew she wanted to reconnect with friends and get out socially on the weekends at least. She knew she wanted to save more money every month to secure her retirement funds. She knew she wanted to go through every box in her home and get rid of everything she no longer wanted or needed. She wanted to be able to come home and relax in the evening, enjoy her peaceful atmosphere, have delicious dinners, engage in activities she loved, and get to bed early.

With The Mid-Life Makeover Method, Alice was able to build a new routine filled with healthy habits one step at a time. She didn't overwhelm herself with a complete overhaul; instead, she set one goal at a time and practiced new ways of showing up in her life until she was solid in her behavior and knew it would stick. Then, she would add another goal and the habits needed to reach it. This process went on for over a year. With every new habit solidified, Alice experienced positive changes.

She felt physically better, more rested, stronger, and thinner. She calmed down considerably, which led to higher-quality sleep. She put up very strong boundaries at work, no longer allowing herself to work well into the evening, take work home, or miss vacations for work. She had routine meetings with her supervisor to keep abreast of the inappropriate workload she had been given and to set different standards for satisfactory performance.

She called old friends and made some new ones, too. She initiated gatherings and enjoyed wine tastings, trips to the countryside, hikes in the woods, and shopping sprees with other women. She joined a calligraphy class and ended up making all her gifts that year while having tons of therapeutic fun in the creative process!

She met with her financial advisor and made specific plans for retirement and started setting aside more money each month. She also mapped out her end-of-life desires, setting up legacy plans for her favorite charities and creating a trust for her assets to be distributed by her lawyer.

Eventually, she made it a habit to sort through one box every week. After a few months, she got through them all and found homes for everything she didn't want, whether it was the garbage can, a recycling center, or Goodwill. She only kept what really mattered to her, put everything in labeled plastic tubs, and bought new shelving to house them all in an orderly fashion. She loved no longer walking around a bunch of dirty cardboard boxes with mysterious contents.

Alice had to face what wasn't working in her life in grand detail. She had to be able to identify the habits that were keeping her from having the life she really wanted, just as she also had to adopt the healthier habits that would support her in living how she wanted to live. As her coach, holding her accountable through-out her makeover as she developed and implemented all these success habits was part of my role and extremely rewarding. I think it's obvious to say that Alice's makeover has helped her love herself fully and live on her own terms. Alice is now enjoying the middle years of her life more than she's ever enjoyed life before. If Alice can do it, so can you!

Write Specific Goals

Earlier in your makeover, you woke up to who you really are and got crystal clear about what you wanted in five areas of your life. One of the best things you can do with this information is to turn those desires into realities by writing specific goals for each thing you want. A goal is a measurement tool that specifies what something will be like once it's reached. For example, you may have said, "I want more money." That's a valid desire, but not a specific goal. If you don't get more specific about that, when you earn even one more dollar, technically, you'll have reached it. Yet, that's likely not what you meant by "more money."

Therefore, you want to lay out every desire in very specific language with a timeline attached to its completion. For example, *I will have an additional $10,000 in my savings account by December 31.* Another example might be, *I will weigh 150 pounds by May 1.* You'll know your goal is written properly when anyone could read it and understand exactly what you want by when.

Just thinking about what your goals are is a great start. However, research indicates that people who write down their goals are far more likely to reach them than those who do not.[8] And those who *read* their written goals daily are

8   Mark Murphy, "Neuroscience Explains Why You Need to Write Down Your Goals if You Actually Want to Achieve Them," Forbes, April 15, 2018, *https://www.forbes.com/sites/markmurphy/2018/04/15/neuroscience-explains-why-you-need-to-write-down-your-goals-if-you-actually-want-to-achieve-them/?sh=499b3cda7905*

even *more* likely to reach their goals than those who do not write them down at all. Reading your goals to yourself every day keeps them in the forefront of your mind, so you're conscious of what you want at all times. Your brain will support you in creating the results as well. You're more likely to see related opportunities or find the resources needed for their completion with these goals always in the forefront of your mind.

Another thing to remember is that you want to create goals that feel possible to you but stretch you as well. For example, if you have the goal to get an engineering degree but you haven't even started college yet, you don't want to write your goal as if you could complete it in the next six weeks. That's not realistic, or even possible. However, you also don't want to write your goal so far out that you can avoid working toward it for a really long time. In other words, you wouldn't want to give yourself fifteen years to get your engineering degree. So, consider realistic but challenging timelines that fit the goals you want to reach. Be fair and honest with yourself about this. You want to set yourself up for success without too much leeway or exception.

Goals keep us on our toes and help us feel inspired to move forward. Life can be very exciting when pursuing goals. But bumps in the road will occur sometimes.

Navigating Road Bumps

When I was in the midst of a year-long professional sabbatical, I decided to fulfill my dream of living by the beach. For four months I rented an upstairs apartment in a house half a block from the ocean in Rehoboth Beach, Delaware. While there, I intended to get in the best physical condition of my life, start dating again, and write a book.

Things started out strong. I joined a gym, hired a personal trainer, and started attending yoga classes regularly. I joined a local writing club and attended the weekly meetings. I started writing my book on my own time as well. I joined a Meetup group and a church to start making friends and meet potential dating partners. I walked along the beach twice a day, every day, and basked in the delight of living by the ocean. My life felt really good, and I was thriving.

Then, three weeks into my beach adventure, as I was coming home from a yoga class one night, I tripped over a concrete parking block, shattered my wrist into nineteen pieces, cut open a knee, put a tiny hole in my other hand, and chipped two teeth. (Yes, this actually happened!) My whole life changed in that moment. Due to my injuries, I could no longer walk along the beach alone, type on the computer, drive, or attend any personal training or gym classes. I decided I wasn't datable either. And, to top it off, even though I'd met about thirty people in my new life and was on a first-name basis with them, my personal trainer was the only person I knew by both first and last name and had contact information for. Every goal I had set for that period of my life was now put on hold, for obvious reasons.

If I can recover from that shock, regroup, and discover ways to find meaning in my life again, so can you if you hit a small or large snag in your goal-reaching process. I ended up spending my time at the beach differently than I'd imagined, but that didn't make it bad.

I decided to take an online course to learn about writing and publishing books. I eventually went back to church and ended up dating a gentleman from there. I still made friends, and whenever I had visitors, they would accompany me on walks along the beach so I could still get some ocean time in. I learned to rest and relax on a whole new level. I cut my stay one month short when I realized my health insurance wasn't covering my medical needs due to being "out of network."

I established new goals as well, mostly related to my recovery. I was supposed to go on a mission trip to Africa just four months after my accident, and one of the requirements was to be able to pull two fifty-pound suitcases behind me on the trip to take supplies to people. Due to my shattered wrist, I was unable to even put my arm behind my back, let alone pull a heavy suitcase anywhere.

My occupational therapist told me to expect a nine-month recovery for full use of my arm, but I told her I didn't have that much time and we had to reach that goal in less than four months. She believed me, and we set specific milestone goals every week, all working toward the ultimate goal of full strength in time for the mission trip. Together, we reached the goal, and I was able to go to Africa and pull the two fifty-pound suitcases behind me!

So, when your goals don't go as planned, you can regroup and establish new goals or tweak your goals to match your newest desires or agenda. Just stay focused on what you really want in your life and always be specific about it. Write your goals down, read them, and verbalize them to others as well if they're not too private. This gives you more energy and momentum for creating everything you want. Plus, when people who care about you know what you're striving for, they will join in encouraging you or providing you with support or resources they may have access to that will get you to your goals even faster.

The Snooze Button and Other No-Nos

It seemed like such a brilliant feature to clockmakers around the world I'm sure, and trust me, I've been grateful for it myself at different stages of my life. I'd be cozily sleeping away on my wood-framed waterbed (yes, this was back in the nineties), buried in the soft sheets, my body floating at perfect rest on top of the warmth of the water below me. I'd be dreaming of walks along the beach hand in hand with my love, the wind blowing my hair behind me and the sun baking on my face, and then the *BEEP! BEEP! BEEP!* would jolt me awake, ripping my perfect peace away and shoving me into the tough reality of the day ahead. *Oh, my! Where's the snooze button? Where's the snooze button? Click. Ok, I've got nine more minutes.* And back under the covers I would go, closing my eyes and pretending I didn't have things to do or places to go.

Then, I would do it all again. Another nine minutes. Another. Another. Until finally, there was no longer time for anything else, like exercise. It was too late. I had to rush around to get cleaned up and ready for the day before the children got up and needed me to get them to school so I could get to work.

When you set specific goals to create what you want in your life, you must examine what habits you have that have kept you from getting what you want so far. For most people, one of their greatest enemies is the snooze button. What else? Want to lose weight? Some would say eating chocolate cake every day instead of reaching for vegetables is counterproductive. Sleeping in every morning instead of getting up early to go to kickboxing class would be another. Heading to the mall every weekend to "shop and lunch" with your sisters or your friends would not exactly support your goal to get out of credit card debt, now would it?

For your mid-life makeover to be successful, you need to take note of any habits you have that block your way to reaching your goals. "Studies by neurobiologists, cognitive psychologists, and others indicate that from 40 to 95 percent of human behavior—how we think, what we say, and our overall actions—falls into the habit category."[9] Habits and routines free up our minds for other things and tend to work in our favor when they're healthy. For example, when you were first learning to drive a car, you probably had to think very consciously about where your hands were on the wheel, how much pressure you were putting on the gas at any given time, and how close you were to the edge of the road. As driving became more of a habit, it no longer required so much concentration. Thus, your mind was free to think about other things.

However, habits can also be very destructive. After a challenging day at work or an uncomfortable conversation with a loved one, you might reach for a glass of wine—or a bottle. You do this because the alcohol numbs you so you no longer feel the negative emotions. The calm created by drinking feels much better than the tension and stress, so the next time you get uncomfortable, you reach for the bottle again. Ultimately, you're avoiding reality and engaging in a dangerous habit that allows you to avoid emotional difficulties and may even develop into an addiction.

Follow yourself around for a day and catch the things you habitually do that may be working against what you really want in the larger picture of your life. Remember the five areas of life we've primarily focused on: health, relationships, finances, professional life, and personal growth. Take stock of your habits in each of those areas.

Let's go back to Alice for a moment. The habits keeping her from the health she wanted included eating fast food regularly, overworking, not exercising, and not getting enough sleep. In her relationships, she wasn't reaching out and connecting with friends because she was overworking, leaving herself little spare time for socializing, and missing vacations. Financially, she wasn't saving for retirement properly and didn't have her estate plans in place yet. Professionally, she was overworking, over-functioning, taking work home with her, not taking proper breaks, letting her colleagues bulldoze her and take her for granted, saying yes to every task presented to her, and not communicating her needs. In terms of her personal development, she was living out of boxes, holding on to things she didn't need, and not leaving herself any time or space to learn new things she was interested in or engage in activities she longed to enjoy.

9   Stuart G. Walesh, "Using the Power of Habits to Work Smarter." Helping You Engineer Your Future. Accessed April 23, 2022. *http://www.helpingyouengineeryourfuture.com/habits-work-smarter.htm*

Ignoring your own needs is one of the worst habits you've likely been engaging in throughout your adult life in the name of caring for others. This is very common in the women I work with. Women tend to find their value and meaning in their relationships, focusing much of their time, energy, resources, and emotion on those they love. This is beautiful on the one hand and destructive on the other. Keeping your balance while taking care of everyone and everything else around you is tricky at best. When you say to yourself or someone else, "I've been meaning to do that for years," you're verbalizing how this habit has played out. The self-neglect is counter to everything you really want. It's far worse than any snooze button could ever be.

So, take stock and be honest. It's all good. Make a list of all the habits you know you need to stop. Dare yourself to stop one of them today. There's no better time to start than right now! You'll be well on your way to solidifying your makeover.

Saying No and Other Absurdities

I'll never forget the look on the camp pastor's face when I said to him the most blasphemous word I could have uttered at the time. I'd spent the past two years planning the week-long annual family church camp with him and a team of other wonderful people. We had held fun, meaningful events for hundreds of people and found great joy and satisfaction in doing so. It was definitely a rewarding experience.

However, my children were young, and this commitment took up so much time and energy. I barely managed it during the two years I was heavily involved. At the end of the second family camp, my children innocently asked me, "Mom, if we come to camp again next summer, will we ever see you?" My heart sank. Here we were at "family camp" and my children and I weren't spending any of the experience together other than sleeping in the same camper. I was too busy running the show; taking care of everyone else; and making sure the meals, classes, safety measures, worship experiences, and everything else was going according to plan.

So, when the camp pastor said, "Will you direct camp again next year?" (which is a year-long commitment that begins right after the last camp ends), I said it—the word, the *blasphemous* word. "No." He looked at me like I had chewed up little children and swallowed them while cackling wickedly. I think he was in shock. Since the day I had met this man, years before, I had never told him no to anything! (It's a good thing he never asked me to jump off a cliff, because I probably would have done it.)

But you know what? He survived. And more importantly, I survived! *And* I began using this horrible, awful word more often. *No!* It's not that hard to say, really. Now, admittedly, he was *not happy* about my decision. He made this very clear and tried to talk me out of it. (And, for the record, he never treated me the same way again.) Now, let's discuss this because I *know* you've had this issue in your life. Besides never telling people no when we need to, another thing women do is worry about what other people think.

My children were a great inspiration for me to be brave enough to be honest and tell him that I had to say no to the opportunity. He responded the same way you've likely had people respond to you when you adopt this very healthy habit of saying no when you need to say no: he didn't like it. Tough! You aren't going to like it if you keep committing to things that don't fit into your world anymore. You'll be drained, frustrated, tired, and angry, and that won't serve anyone.

You may even lose people over your nos. That's okay. I lost the friendship, admiration, and camaraderie I had with that pastor, and I felt that loss for a while. But then I realized that if he were a true friend of mine and loved me as much as he professed to, he would've accepted my answer and me, just as I am. But he didn't. That's not the kind of friendship I want in my life. A true friend will stick by you even when you disappoint them. They will strive to understand even when they don't agree with you. And guess what? The next time they need something and think you might be a good fit, they will ask you again.

Saying no is just one of the thousands of awesome habits you can begin to incorporate into your life to replace the destructive ones you have identified thus far that are keeping you from the life you want.

Let's go back to dear Alice again. One by one, she adopted healthy habits to get her life where she wanted it to be. She started putting strong boundaries around her time at work, leaving at the end of an eight-hour shift whether the work was complete or not. She bought groceries on the weekends and did lots of cooking on Sundays so she could pack healthy meals for lunch and quickly heat up good, nutritious meals for dinner when she returned home from work.

She started calling her friends and initiating get-togethers. She went out for walks at night after work whenever the weather cooperated. She spent time regularly going through one box after another to free up space and get organized, keeping only what mattered to her. She joined an exercise class and a calligraphy class. She made time for fun every weekend. She even went on vacations every quarter and turned off the notifications on her phone about work emails so she wasn't tempted to check on things while away.

Putting all these healthy habits in place turned Alice's life around. You can do the same for yourself. Look back on your list of destructive habits and spend some time considering what healthy habits you could incorporate to replace them. Give yourself all kinds of yummy options. Once you have ideas, pace yourself, as most of us succeed more easily if we change only one or two things at a time. Then you can put systems in place to support you in really solidifying your new choices.

Tip the Scales in Your Favor

Truth time. I love to read. I mean, I sincerely love to read. But I have stacks of books I've purchased and have yet to read. This has been true of me for a long time. I read, but not as much as I would like to. Why? Because I haven't incorporated it into my daily routine consistently. The kind of reading I do supports my personal development and my business. I eat up self-help, self-development, motivational, inspirational, and business-building books. I use them constantly in my work and in my life. It's also very stimulating and entertaining to me. Every time I read, I feel like I'm growing, and I really like that!

I also live by my calendar. Everything I need to do, want to do, or have scheduled to do, I put in there. I think I would be lost without it. So, it occurred to me one day to put "Read" in my schedule. What a brilliant idea! "Read." Monday: Read. Tuesday: Read. Every day: Read. Read, Cindy. *Read!* Putting this in my calendar made it more of a commitment to myself. I trust my calendar. I live by it. Therefore, I'm reading more and more and loving it!

So, I recommend you start to put down in your calendar, on your whiteboard, or wherever you keep track of things, the daily habits you want to incorporate. Put it on the list in your planner just like you would a doctor's appointment or a board meeting. Then, you'll do it! Maybe it's a spin class; maybe it's a hike; or maybe it's taking your multivitamin, practicing your speech, or weeding the garden. I don't care if it's picking your nose—get it on the calendar now to set yourself up for greater follow-through.

Another thing you can do to set yourself up for success with your new habits and goal-reaching efforts is to tell people close to you what you're striving to do. Let them know what your goals are and the new habits you're engaging in. Give them permission to ask you how it's going. They may have tips for you or know of additional resources that would support you. They can also offer additional encouragement and accountability.

Reward yourself every time you choose a new habit as well. Be careful with this one, though. If your goal is to eat healthier to keep your cholesterol under control, once you've had the veggies, don't reward yourself with ice cream! But when you decide to call a friend to vent about a problem instead of reaching for a cigarette to cope, give yourself a pat on the back for the healthier choice and treat yourself to something simple but nice. Maybe a movie you've been wanting to see. Maybe you take a longer lunch break to relax. Whatever! Celebrating your wins is further positive reinforcement for your efforts, which solidifies those healthier habits for good. This will get you to your goals quicker too.

You could also hire a support person who can help you incorporate the new habit. You could get a financial advisor if you're working on positive money habits. You could hire a personal trainer to help you with your new workout schedule. You could find an addiction counselor to help you find alternatives to drinking alcohol. You could hire a coach (me!) to help you write your goals, map out the healthy habits needed to reach them, and hold you accountable to them until they're completely ingrained in your daily life.

Don't Forget Your Beliefs

Keep your belief systems in check throughout this process. Remember the T.F.A. Cycle? Your thoughts lead to your feelings, which lead to your actions. Make sure you're mastering your mindset and thinking properly about your habits and goals to keep yourself on track. If you have a rough day you may be tempted to believe, *I can't do it another day.* If you go there in your head, it's important that you catch yourself and challenge that thought. Is it *really* true that you literally can't go another day? Or is this just a particularly tough one? What else could be true?

Check your thoughts and reframe them to support you in getting back on track with your habits and goals.

When the daily grind of it all starts to get old and your energy is running particularly low, remember the big picture of what you want. Sometimes, when you incorporate new habits, you don't necessarily see direct, obvious results right away. These might take a while to appear. Be patient. Remember what you want.

For example, maybe you're buried in debt, but you want to save for a car. You cut corners in your expenses, use coupons, watch for sales, stop all unnecessary spending, and put all your extra money toward the credit card balance. Yet, it looks like you've barely put a dent in it. Look again, and don't be discouraged. Perhaps you decreased the balance by $400. That's significant, even if you still have $2,600 to go! With the big picture in mind, that's an amazing start! Even not *adding* to the debt over a month's time is a victory, let alone cutting out that much of it. Always keep your perspective in your favor to keep yourself inspired to continue striving for what you want.

If you're so inclined, you could also engage in any spiritual practices you enjoy as an additional approach and support system. Perhaps you believe in the power of prayer. Maybe you find solace in silence or meditation. Maybe reading scriptures or other inspirational texts strengthens you. Going to church, temple, or support groups of other kinds may really give you additional doses of love, empowerment, and belief in your ability to accomplish everything you've identified to be of importance. Connecting to that bigger, wiser part of you that has inner knowledge will offer you guidance, comfort, and inspiration to stay on your best path.

Visualizing the results you have in mind—seeing them as a detailed movie in your head—will also add a secret sauce to bringing your habits into your daily life more naturally and easily.

Ninety-Nine Percent Isn't Good Enough

I can imagine what you're thinking right now. Cindy, are you *crazy*? What are you, some kind of sick perfectionist who has no grip on reality whatsoever? (The answer to both of those questions is *no*, by the way.) Let me explain.

According to Jack Canfield, "In life, the spoils of victory go to those who make a 100% commitment to the outcome, to those who have a 'no matter what it takes' attitude. Once you make a 100% commitment to something, there are no exceptions. It's a done deal."[10]

The truth is a total commitment to clarity. You know what you want, and you live by that. It's much simpler than being wishy-washy. Think of the times you've been uncertain about a decision. You do want the job, in a way, but in another, you don't. On the one hand, you do want to date this person, but on the other hand, you're not sure you're compatible. You feel like you should weigh less, but you know your personal worth has nothing to do with your body size. You're leaning toward cutting off that toxic friend, but your religious beliefs encourage you to love, forgive, and be kind. These are all conflicting thoughts and emotions that leave you dangling between more than one option.

When you make a solid decision to stay laser-focused 100 percent of the time, you will experience incredible results. You won't be easily swayed off the path or distracted by anything that doesn't fit into your new habits and lifestyle. You will be clear about what you will and will not do.

Canfield shares another perspective regarding performing 99.9 percent versus 100 percent of the time:

Consider what a commitment to just 99.9% quality would mean in the following work situations. It would mean . . .
- 2 unsafe landings at O'Hare International Airport each day
- 16,000 lost pieces of mail per hour
- 20,000 incorrectly filled drug prescriptions every year
- 500 incorrect surgical operations performed each week
- 50 newborn babies dropped at birth by doctors every day
- 22,000 checks deducted from the wrong account each hour
- Your heart failing to beat 32,000 times each year[11]

All of a sudden, that 0.1 percent really makes a difference, doesn't it? So, think about it for yourself, your goals, your habits, and everything you've declared you want in your mid-life makeover. Loving yourself fully and living on your terms doesn't include sort of reaching your goals, getting partially there, or living a life

---

10   Canfield, *The Success Principles*™, 251
11   Canfield, *The Success Principles*™, 253-254

of mediocrity. You won't feel gratified by kind of getting healthier, sort of saving for retirement, enjoying your partner somewhat, feeling so-so at work, or doing only a little of what you've always wanted to do. Imagine what your life would look like now if you gave it your all? What other priority have you ever had that could be more important than a 100 percent commitment to yourself?

Buddha, I Am Not

When your life is crumbling, as mine was in my early forties, you can reach the point of being willing to try anything, even something that seems far-fetched or ridiculous at first. During a personal and professional development training I attended as my life was imploding, I learned about creating a "power hour" for yourself every day. The idea was to spend one hour every day on habits that started you on a great path for the rest of the day to be as positive, productive, and joy filled as possible.

The primary suggestions were to write in a gratitude journal, meditate, and exercise. Other ideas included prayer time, music therapy, creative time, reading something inspirational, doing affirmations, yoga, stretching, or breath work. I already had an exercise routine going for another time of day, so I thought I'd start with inspirational reading, gratitude journaling, and meditation. (I had never meditated before, but why the heck not?)

I set my alarm, inspiring books stacked on my bedside table and a new journal and pen in the drawer. The next morning when my alarm went off, I didn't push the snooze button but instead picked a book and read for twenty minutes. Then, I opened my new journal and wrote at the top of the page, "I am so happy and grateful for_____" and listed five things I was uniquely thankful for that I had been aware of or experienced in the last twenty-four hours. Even though I was going through so much at the time, I found this pretty simple. Next, it was time to meditate.

I put the book, the journal, and the pen away. I shut off the little bedside lamp, so the room was dark and quiet. I lowered my eyes and kept breathing. In. Out. In. Out. *I wonder what the weather is going to be like today.* (Oops.) In. Out. In. My cat, Taboo, jumped onto my lap. She landed pretty abruptly, and I realized how full my bladder was. In. Out. *Oh boy, this isn't going well. What am I supposed to be doing? I have to go to the bathroom.*

I don't remember how many mornings it took for me to really sink into the wonderful experience of meditation, but day after day, week after week, no matter how distracted I got or how silly I felt, I just kept showing up and doing my best. I stayed 100 percent committed to the idea of a power hour to strengthen myself and my life, and eventually, it truly paid off.

I was going through hell in my life and was unsure how the future would unfold for me and my family or if my hopes and dreams for myself could ever come true. But through this newly engrained daily routine of reading inspirational material, writing in my gratitude journal, and meditating, I calmed down; trusted life more; and let it unfold without as much stress, worry, or need to control the universe. I found myself getting inspired with new ideas and having visions of a better life. I could see a better future ahead of me. I took solace in knowing something bigger than me had my back—all of our backs—and that I could trust life to unfold in ways that would work for everyone, and I didn't have to sweat the details.

Now *that*, my friends, is power. What a game-changer! My personal makeover began with greater awareness of my own contribution to my life, continued with more clearly defined desires, and became a tangible reality when I found healthy habits to replace the destructive ones—taking solid action to create the life I knew I wanted and needed. The power hour catapulted me forward so much that, to this day, I still practice it very consistently. Sometimes, when on vacation, I slip out of the routine, and if more than a few days go by, I start to really feel the difference emotionally.

Once you begin to love yourself fully, you'll feel the negative effects if you get off track. Right now, that may be difficult to believe, but it's so true. Stay the course! Give it your all! You're worth the 100 percent commitment!

Key Takeaways

- Goals need to be specific and measurable to be effective.
- Goals should be realistic but also stretch you.
- Writing your goals down and reading them daily greatly increases the likelihood of reaching them.
- Habits can be destructive or constructive in terms of reaching your goals.

- You can replace destructive habits with new, healthy habits.
- There are many ways to increase your success rate by incorporating good habits into your daily routines.
- Ninety-nine percent isn't good enough—make a 100 percent commitment to your makeover!
- Creating a daily power hour unique to you can catapult your success.

Now It's Your Turn: The Habit Check

List out all the areas of your life you've focused on throughout this book for your mid-life makeover. The primary areas mentioned in the book are health, relationships, finances, professional life, and personal growth. For each area, write at least one goal you have for your makeover. Then, for each goal, list habits you know you need to stop and habits you know you need to start to reach those goals.

Coming Up Next . . .

Now that you have specific goals in front of you and a plan to incorporate healthy habits to reach them, it's time to create a sustainability plan so you can keep up with the life you're now living. You'll learn the best practices for maintaining your new lifestyle, including how to be the leader in your own life and how to surround yourself with a strong support team.

Chapter Nine

Keeping It Up!

ALL OF LYNN'S COACHING WORK WAS FINALLY PAYING OFF. SHE SAT ON HER COZY white couch, curled up in her peach-colored bathrobe and fuzzy white slippers, a cup of herbal mint tea warming her hands. Breathing a sigh of relief, she looked around her newly decorated living room, enjoying the photograph she had taken of the Smoky Mountains at sunset, which hung majestically in a thick, rustic wood frame on the wall opposite where she was sitting.

She loved her bay window, which offered a stunning view of trees and a wide-open space that invited her to join in later for a walk in the fresh, crisp air. Finally, she was living how she wanted to live, where she wanted to live. Having bought the aged property herself, Lynn had known it would take time to turn it into her personal sanctuary, but she had done it. The space inside and out felt like her own.

Even the clutter was gone at last. Having a habit of keeping everything can create stacks, piles, and chaos by mid-life. In addition to a lifetime of emotional baggage, Lynn had transferred her physical clutter to the old (new) home as well. When her husband had died four years before, she could hardly imagine the day she would part with his things, but she had managed to do it, along with every-thing else she no longer wanted, needed, or loved.

Prone to shopping when she felt anxious or alone, Lynn easily accumulated things she really didn't need or want. However, through our coaching together, she learned new ways of managing her emotional challenges and didn't resort to malls, credit cards, or retail therapy any longer. She could finally sit still in her grief, be reasonably comfortable with the silence, allow the tears to flow, and find solace.

Gradually, she made new friends, who were mostly other widows, through a grief support group nearby. They became like sisters and started to do things together outside of the formal group sessions. Her life felt full again, but in a balanced way.

One of her greatest lessons learned from being widowed was realizing she didn't need to do everything on her own. She realized it was okay to ask for help or even hire help to accomplish the tasks she wanted to be completed. Shifting from a "we" mentality to an "I" mentality was one of her most uncomfortable tasks as she had been married for thirty-seven years, always considering him in any decision, right down to what groceries to put on the list every week.

When Lynn came looking for my help, she said, "I know I don't have to do everything by myself. I can do anything I put my mind to. I can create a different life for myself. It's okay to hire someone to keep me accountable and to be my support system." As she grew and changed through our teamwork, Lynn reached the point where she was ready to move on. Her makeover complete, she was ready to venture out all on her own.

Completing your makeover from the inside out is much like preparing for a marathon. You train for months, building your strength, adding to your miles, and changing your eating, drinking, and sleeping schedule to accommodate what you're asking your body to do. You continue to build on your new talents, skills, and endurance. You change your habits to reach the goal.

Then the day comes for the race. You've arrived. It's time to implement everything you've learned to get to this moment. You want to be able to keep up what you've built and sustain yourself throughout the marathon.

The marathon of mid-life is no different, really. Throughout the makeover, you've built new skills and new ways of thinking, feeling, and acting. You've found the best ways to create what you declared you wanted in your life through new success habits incorporated into your daily routine. You've let go of everything that doesn't serve you in completing the race of your life.

After all you've done to change your life for the better, nothing would be more disappointing than returning to your old ways of thinking, destructive ways of being, and inability to follow through with your dreams. This is why the final step, Keeping It Up, is all about establishing a rock-solid sustainability plan to move you into your future with confidence and excitement.

Whatever You Say, Jack!

I once went to Maui, though I didn't see Maui except for the airport, the ride to and from the airport, and out the seaside windows of Jack Canfield's private home and training center. I was there with nineteen other strangers from all over the country who were trainees like me, as well as four prominent leaders in the self-development movement and additional support staff for a four-day private retreat.

One afternoon, we were sitting in groups of six doing a mastermind activity, and I was fortunate to have Jack in the chair next to mine. We were going around the circle and sharing our goals and what challenges we were experiencing in our lives as we were attempting to reach them.

When my turn came, I spent the majority of my few minutes explaining how my husband had held me back from starting my own business and other priorities I had. I explained how he criticized my dreams and kept me stuck by expecting me to put his agenda ahead of all others and be satisfied doing so. After politely listening to my soliloquy of blaming and complaining about my spouse, Jack turned to me, looked me in the eyes, and said, "Cindy, it is your job to live your life."

I think the clouds must have split open and the angels sang loudly or something because my spine tingled, the hair stood up on my neck, and my stomach flopped. As non-profound as those words may seem to you, they hit me in the heart like the biggest wake-up call you could ever imagine.

Oh my gosh, it *is* my job to live my life! Why was I just living his? I mean, I did love the guy, and we had two children together, but wow, *I am a person!*

I knew what Jack was saying. He was asking me to be the leader of my own life, just as I am now encouraging you to do. That's how I want you to look at yourself from this moment on.

Being the leader of your own life means taking total responsibility for everything that happens and doesn't happen. The best leaders don't waste time (like I was) pointing their fingers at other people for their problems or complaining about situations outside of their control. Rather, they focus on where they have the ability to make a difference, and that's in their own choices, actions, inactions, thoughts, ideas, and feelings.

Leaders are difference-makers. Leaders hold a strong vision for their lives and actively pursue the manifestation of it. Leaders learn from their experiences and use times that feel like bumps in the road as feedback to redirect them to a more productive path. When challenging circumstances arrive, they don't hide or give up; instead, they become problem-solvers, determined to overcome whatever is attempting to get in their way. They thrive on their own energy and have the confidence to stay persistent during the most turbulent storms life can offer.

According to writer Sarmad Hassan, great leaders have the following qualities: integrity, confidence, focus, determination, commitment, strong decision-making skills, good communication skills, passion, and empowerment.[12] Imagine how well you could sustain your mid-life makeover if you embodied each and every one of these qualities! There isn't any reason in the world you can't.

After that bulldozer of a message I received from Jack, I began to take full responsibility for myself and became the CEO of my life. Of course, there was resistance from others who had a vested interest in keeping me small and in the background of my own life, but to be truly happy, I knew I needed to love myself fully and live on my own terms. No one else could do that for me. I had to take the lead.

Stepping into Queendom

Queens are regal, sophisticated leaders of their land. They sit high on their thrones, looking out over the kingdom they rule with grace and confidence. They're kind, yet assertive. They're forgiving, yet hold high standards for themselves and those around them. They keep a tight circle of close people and confidantes while mixing with many for the greater good of all.

Being the leader of your own life as you go forward means stepping into your role as queen of your kingdom. You'll make wise decisions that benefit you and those around you. You'll be respectful to all but close to few. Your boundaries will be clear. You'll be a class act everywhere you go and bask in the privacy and comfort of your own domain. Few will know you intimately enough to understand you, and you'll be judged for who you are, but you'll be confident enough that this won't deter you from living how you feel is best.

Here are four ways to build confidence in your leadership of your own life:

---

12   Sarmad Hassan, "Top 15 Leadership Qualities That Make Good Leaders (2022)," Taskque, January 5, 2022, *https://blog.taskque.com/characteristics-good-leaders/*.

1. Create space to be efficient, focused, comfortable, and sit in your power.
2. Stay updated on information, stay open to learning, and remain a student of life.
3. Exude optimism, passion, and commitment to everything you believe in.
4. Show up physically with confidence—a.k.a. making eye contact, having a strong handshake, smiling, walking tall with shoulders back, and entering a room with respect and grace.

When you implement these tips, others will respond accordingly, believing you are the queen of your life just as you desire to be. And most importantly, *you* will believe it! Now, you just need to sustain all you've built.

Sustainability for Dummies: Eleven Steps

As the newly crowned queen of your life, you'll want to incorporate these strategies to sustain all the changes you've made throughout your makeover. Here are eleven steps to sustainability:

1. Stay awake. This means keeping yourself in check and recognizing how you're showing up in your life and how you're not.
2. Focus on yourself. This is about your own behaviors, choices, and decisions, not other people's. Focusing on others is distracting and disempowering. When you're tempted to stray into those areas, quickly regroup with yourself.
3. Love and appreciate yourself at all times, no matter what! You are human, and you have made a lot of adjustments in your life. You may find yourself falling backward in your thoughts or sliding back into an old habit. Give yourself compassion when you realize this and then move on.
4. Track your successes. Nothing is more empowering or encouraging than experiencing success, so do frequent check-ins about what's working well. The strengths you find in yourself by doing this can also be utilized to move you forward during rougher times.
5. Strive to feel good. Keep your vibration high. Feeling good as often as possible is a valid goal and a wonderful state of being to build from. When you feel good, you're far more likely to make clear decisions and delight in the journey you're on.

6. Remain clear. Keep your eyes on the prize, so to speak. Remember to stay focused on everything you said you wanted. If your desires change, that's okay. Adjust your life to accommodate new desires any time they arise. You are the key visionary of your life, so you must hold the vision for it to be realized.

7. Let go of the unnecessary. Let go of anything that gets in the way of the life you really want. Yes, you eliminated a lot of energy drainers earlier in your makeover, but these tend to pop up on a regular basis for most people, so stay aware of any obstacles and quickly remove them to keep your positive flow.

8. Think properly. This is your greatest sustainability strategy! Keep your thoughts in check by remembering how important the nature of your thoughts is in either supporting you on a positive path or dismantling you with negativity. You're either an inner critic or an inner coach—your choice! When fears show up, question their validity, and find new ways to observe any situation. How you speak to yourself about anything will be a determining factor in its sustainability.

9. Forgive yourself quickly when you fall short. Find your compassionate self when responding to whatever didn't go as you had hoped, and begin again. When you can let go by forgiving yourself, you leave the past behind and start fresh. You allow your human self to recover and regroup, ready for the next thing.

10. Learn valuable lessons along the way. Keep an open mind and think of all you've gained throughout your journey. See the hidden treasures in everything you've done and everywhere you've been. Use this as encouragement to keep going.

11. Continue to invest in yourself. Open yourself up to new experiences, people, opportunities, resources, ideas, strategies, and anyone or anything else that can support you in manifesting anything and everything you've always wanted. My client Lynn did all of these things to keep her life moving in the direction she wanted to go, and the rewards have been immense. Her persistence, along with the accountability of regular coaching, paid off.

What a Caterpillar in the Arctic Circle Can Teach Us

Within the first year of having my online coaching business, I decided it was time to create an automated webinar. Not being the most technical girl on the block, I had a lot to learn. Many times, I found myself frustrated with this button or that link and would come to the point of wanting to pull my hair out, give up, and go work at a coffee shop or something. I remember thinking, *I am a reasonably intelligent human being . . . why can't I figure out how to edit these slides in my Haiku Deck? And how come I can't seem to get this video downloaded or uploaded or saved (or whatever) in StealthSeminar, especially after watching their "easy-to-use" instructional videos?* Maddening. Crazy-making. Was it worth all of this?

After another grueling day of webinar construction, I curled up to snuggle on the couch with my beloved and watch *Planet Earth.* The episode was about creatures of the Arctic Circle, one of the coldest places on Earth. Although I was a bit tired and could have easily fallen asleep, all cozy and warm, I was captivated by the best story of persistence I had ever heard.

There are caterpillars living in the Arctic Circle, hidden under rocks. In the spring, they come out after everything has melted and eat everything they can for three months. Then, with full, satisfied stomachs, they crawl back under a rock and curl up for nine months of hibernation. *Nine months!* Nine months of snow, ice, and freezing temperatures that you and I cannot even imagine! This three-inch little creature freezes over and lays there for three-quarters of the year, waiting for the next thaw.

And then, after everything has melted and spring has sprung, out comes the caterpillar again, eating for three months and then crawling back under the rock to freeze and hibernate *again.*

This tiny, miraculous creature does this for fourteen years! *Fourteen!* (Does it have a piece of paper and a pencil under there to keep track?) Scientists say they go through this routine for fourteen years, and *then,* the next time they come out from under the rock, they create a chrysalis and become a moth! In a very brief period of time, they mate, reproduce, and then fly away!

I've never heard such an amazing story of persistence in my life, seriously. I can hardly believe it to this day! So, after hearing that story, I thought, *Well, if the little caterpillar can do all that, surely I can get my webinar done.* (If you'd like to watch the webinar, it's called "The Five Key Shifts to Becoming An Unstoppable,

Confident Woman Who Knows What She Wants & How To Get It" and you can access it here for free: *www.cindydwhitmer.com/fivekeyshifts*. If you like it, you have me and the caterpillar to thank!)

Seriously though, if a caterpillar can manage that lifestyle for that long *and* survive *and* end up producing more life, you can rock your own mid-life makeover, no matter what challenges you've faced or what you've experienced up until now!

Author and researcher Brené Brown teaches about resiliency. She says, "Resilience is the ability to overcome adversity."[13] In her book *The Gifts of Imperfection*, she shares research that indicates five common factors of resilient people:

1. They are resourceful and have good problem-solving skills.
2. They are more likely to seek help.
3. They hold the belief that they can do something that will help them to manage their feelings and cope.
4. They have social support available to them.
5. They are connected with others, such as family or friends.[14]

Brown also goes a step further, discussing the importance of hope along with resiliency:

Hope is not an emotion; it's a way of thinking or a cognitive process. Hope happens when,

1. We have the ability to set realistic goals. (I know where I want to go.)
2. We are able to figure out how to achieve those goals, including the ability to stay flexible and develop alternative routes. (I know how to get there, I'm persistent, and I can tolerate disappointment and try again.)
3. We believe in ourselves. (I can do this.)[15]

Hope, according to Brown, is "a combination of setting goals, having the tenacity and perseverance to pursue them, and believing in our own abilities."[16]

---

13 Brené Brown, *The Gifts of Imperfection: Let Go of Who You Think You're Supposed to Be and Embrace Who You Are* (Center City, MN: Hazelden Publishing, 2010), 63.
14 Brown, *The Gifts of Imperfection*, 64.
15 Brown, *The Gifts of Imperfection*, 65.
16 Brown, *The Gifts of Imperfection*, 66.

Key Takeaways

- Being the leader of your own life means taking total responsibility for everything that happens and doesn't happen.
- The best leaders don't waste time (like I did) pointing their fingers at other people for their problems or complaining about situations outside of their control.
- Leaders learn from their experiences and use times that feel like bumps in the road as feedback to redirect them to a more productive path.
- Being the leader of your own life as you go forward means stepping into your role as queen of your kingdom.
- You should incorporate sustainable strategies to maintain all the changes you have made throughout your makeover.
- Open yourself up to new experiences, people, opportunities, resources, ideas, strategies, and anyone or anything else that can support you in manifesting anything and everything you've always wanted.
- Brené Brown teaches how resiliency and hope play significant roles in our persistence and sustainability, no matter what our goals or desires are.

Now It's Your Turn: Create Your Team

Considering all the changes you've made throughout your makeover and the ones you continue to evolve in, what people could be significant players in providing you with emotional support, spiritual strength, further education, training, or accountability? List the top five people you have a personal relationship with who could be great encouragers, listeners, and providers of support and strength for you to sustain your makeover lifestyle. Consult with your spiritual teachers, such as a minister, guru, rabbi, or priest. List any professionals you may wish to hire to be a part of your team of continued learning, evolution, or accountability. Examples include a nutritionist, a financial advisor, a coach (me!), a personal trainer, a naturopath, a therapist, a doctor, etc. Start connecting with people and engaging them in your growth by asking for what you need.

It's Not Hip-Hop; It's a Wrap!

So far, your mid-life makeover has included:

- Understanding who you are, how you've shown up, and the roles and responsibilities you've played in your life.
- Clarifying everything you ideally want and identifying the gap between where you are now and where you're going.
- Letting go of anything and everything you no longer need, want, or use.
- Cleaning up your messes, incompletes, and tolerations.
- Creating space for the "new" in your life.
- Turning your mind into your new best friend.
  - Learning how to speak to yourself and about yourself properly.
  - Knowing how to dismantle your fears.
  - Reframing thoughts that cause you suffering.
  - Focusing on what you want to grow in your life.
  - Finding words to soothe yourself when you're triggered.
- Releasing old habits and developing new ones to support the life you want.
- Planning your daily routines around creating a joy-filled, meaningful life.
- Being in charge of yourself and standing strong in self-leadership.

Notice how good you feel and how energizing it is to have changed the dynamics and the details of your previously difficult life.

Coming Up Next . . .

Now that you have a strong sustainability plan in place, we'll reiterate the importance of being the leader in your own life and identify what tangible evidence to look for that indicates you're succeeding in doing just that.

Chapter Ten

Nancy Drew It

YOU MUST TAKE TOTAL RESPONSIBILITY FOR YOUR LIFE. THIS IS WHERE YOUR POWER lies. Above all, you must learn to love yourself fully, without apology or hesitation. Once you grasp that and embrace yourself, you can move through your makeover, creating the life you want and living fully within it. You will, at last, be happier than you've ever been!

There's no better time than right now to get started! Mid-life doesn't have to be an unsettling, crazy time that just transitions into old age, deterioration, and death. It's not all downhill from here unless you decide it is. Instead, mid-life can be the best years of your life so far! It's your choice, every time!

So, let's "Nancy Drew" this. Let's be the detectives of our own lives. Tangible evidence of your successful makeover will look something like this:

- You put yourself first when making choices or decisions because you now know what's best for you will also be best for everyone around you.
- You approach life with greater confidence, i.e., trying new things, saying no, telling the truth, asking for what you need, and investing in yourself to create your ideal life.
- Your relationships are healthier and feel encouraging, fun, and mutually satisfying. You've reduced or eliminated toxic relationships. You've incorporated strong boundaries.
- You feel clear about how you want your life to look in every area and base your decisions on aligning with those things.
- You let go of everything that doesn't align with that vision, reducing your overwhelm in life.
- You feel more organized and can find anything you need at any time.

- Your life runs like a well-oiled machine; everything functions properly, time management is no longer a problem, and you keep up with your to-do lists easily.
- You speak kindly to yourself, like you would a loved one.
- You face your fears with greater compassion, understanding, and skills in order to move forward despite them.
- Your life is no longer consumed with anxiety and worry because you've adopted new beliefs that provide a sense of calm, peace, and trust.
- Your emotional reactivity is way down because you understand your triggers and can separate your past from your present, handling anything that comes your way with less stress and more ease.
- You've created a daily routine filled with activities that feel good to you and support your holistic health, such as exercise or movement; mindful eating; regular sleep; rest and relaxation; and spiritual nourishment like reading, prayer, meditation, breath work, gratitude journaling, music, creativity, positive outlets, and play.
- You sustain yourself by taking charge of your life, your desires, and your health; others no longer run your show.
- You invest in yourself through personal or professional development of your own choosing.
- You surround yourself with a strong support system including friends, family, colleagues, mentors, teachers, coaches, and others who provide accountability and guidance as you continue to grow and evolve on your terms.

Like every woman you've met in this book, you'll learn to love yourself and live on your terms. Mid-life will be a time of great joy, abundant health, vibrant living, great purpose, personal freedom, positive relationships, and exciting growth. You'll find yourself feeling so good and looking forward to more!

My Fifteen-Thousand-Mile Journey

When both my children left home after high school, I was ready to leave as well. I had anticipated this new season of my life for some time. I knew I was burned-out at work, I knew I was ready for a new community to call home, and I knew

I needed to take a deep breath about what I wanted the next phase of my life to look like. I was no longer tied to anyone or anything, and I was curious to find out what was next for me.

What I did know for sure was that I wanted a midsize university town to live in that celebrated diversity and had lots of live music, art, culture, a strong presence of outdoor life and recreation, and spiritual communities I resonated with.

I knew I wanted to start my own full-time private coaching, speaking, and writing practice. I had worked for other organizations throughout my career and had done side gigs on top of that, but I wanted to venture out completely on my own.

And I knew I wanted to find love. Healthy love. The relationship with a great companion I always felt I was capable of creating but just couldn't in the context of my marriage.

But where would all of these parts of my makeover come together? I didn't know for sure, so I quit my job, put my house up for sale, packed my car, took my kids off to each of their colleges, and then started out on what ended up being a fifteen-thousand-mile road trip through twenty-eight states over the course of a year. I visited friends and family all over, checked out communities that met my criteria, and asked for spiritual guidance every step of the way.

My adventures were many, too many to spell out here, but through it all, I got to know more about who I was, what I wanted, what I needed, and how to align myself in the best environment to fulfill my calling in the next stage of my life.

If you can work it out to give yourself the gift of time and space on a larger level than a weekend getaway or a retreat, I highly encourage you to do so. I spent hours and hours and hours alone, contemplating every question life presents us. I learned to keep the good company of myself, even as I was reconnecting with loved ones all over the country. It was one of the greatest acts of self-love I had ever allowed myself, and it led me to the fulfillment of so many dreams I'd had for so long.

This is what a mid-life makeover can look and feel like, going outside the box and making decisions that some may think are not only nontraditional but downright crazy! I spent almost an entire year not working, spent money funding the trip as well as maintaining a home that wouldn't sell, and chose to view it all as a wonderful investment in my future. Indeed, it was.

I spent time with people who affirmed what I was doing. I shared my experiences and my hopes for the future with them. I felt uplifted everywhere I went. I made a conscious effort to contribute something positive to each place I visited, leaving a loving mark on those who had joined me on the journey.

Fast-forward to the following autumn. I had chosen my new community, which was, ironically, only fifty-five miles from the one I had lived in for the previous ten years. I told myself I would move once my house was sold. Then, one day I was walking back into my little post-divorce home (the place the kids and I affectionately called "The Cottage") from the mailbox, sifting through the envelopes, when I heard a voice say, *You're moving before your house sells, sooner than you think.* And I said back to the voice, *Well, that would be stupid and makes no sense.* End of conversation.

Two days later, a friend of mine called and said her home (in the same town) had sold suddenly, and they needed to get out of their house but had to live somewhere in town until the following summer when their youngest child graduated from high school. She wanted to know if I would give them a reference so they could rent something in the meantime. I said I certainly could, but that I wished they felt my house would be a good alternative for them. She said, "We thought about that but didn't want to rush you to move." (How funny—I was *more than ready* and couldn't be rushed!)

Within the next five days, I had become their landlord, getting a formal rental agreement ready based on our mutually agreed upon terms, *and* I had contacted several landlords in my future community, looked at ten properties in one day, and signed a contract for the one I had viewed first (and knew instinctively all day long was the one).

One month later, I was in my new condo in my new town. Within two months, I was actively building up my new business and had joined two networking groups, gotten involved heavily in community life, and started dating again.

Did I mention I bought myself a new bed, too? When I got divorced, I took the old guest bed to be my bed. You know, the bed my former in-laws gave us twenty-some years before, which was old even then? The bed that became the family sickbed when someone needed separate quarters to overcome an illness. The bed everyone who was ever a guest in our house slept in. I mean, this bed was *old.* Not to mention the fact that there was no headboard anymore, and shortly after the kids and I moved out, my son jumped on it really hard and broke one of the legs. I had stacked bricks to replace the broken leg, not having any extra money to spend at that time.

Having learned to love myself fully at last, I decided it was time for a bed suitable for a queen. Even though the last thing I needed to be doing was spending more money "unnecessarily" that year, I bought myself a lovely new bed with no history, no memories, no stains, no brokenness, no nothing. Everything new. I even chose a queen-size one, telling myself it was a bed made for a queen—*me!* I bought all new bedding as well: fresh sheets, new pillows, a new bedspread, decorative pillows, the works. It's beautiful and extremely comfortable. I went to bed every night feeling like a queen, and that's a pretty great way to end every day! And then, I asked God to send me one man to share it with someday. Just one.

Within six months of arriving in my new community, I met the man with whom I continue to have the most loving, fun, healthy relationship I have ever experienced in my life. When he asked me to move in with him, I told him the bed story and insisted we would sleep in this bed—and we do to this day.

All the major pieces of my mid-life makeover came together through this transition. When you know who you are, you get crystal clear about what you want, you eliminate what no longer aligns with you, make your mind your best friend, and develop new success habits, life will believe you and provide you with the way to make everything possible. I'm not special compared to other women. I just knew how to do the work, and now I teach others how to do so as well.

Chapter Eleven

Your Strong Start Is Only the Beginning

AS I WRITE THIS NOW, I REALIZE THAT TEN YEARS AGO ON THIS VERY DAY, I FILED FOR divorce. At that time, over a year had passed since Jack Canfield had looked me in the eyes and said, "Cindy, it is your job to live your life." My mid-life makeover was only just beginning then. So much change was ahead of me, and there was a mysterious quality to my unknown future. Yet, I was hopeful, even in the midst of total despair.

My mid-life makeover took many turns—as they can—and trickled ultimately into every area of my life. In the next few years, I also endured my father's sudden death, a beloved pet's disappearance, two broken wrists and surgeries at two separate times and places, totaling my car from hitting a deer, an empty nest, moving, and a career transformation. Life just kept coming and evolving.

Now I'm sitting at my desk, which has the words *Dream Big* painted across it. I'm gazing out my home office window at the hummingbird feeder, wind chimes, and shells hanging off the deck floor above, all swaying in the light November breeze. The chimes are sounding ever so slightly, like a gentle, steady reminder that my life is good and peaceful, and I can count on my heart to keep beating without having to think about it or guide it along.

The winding stone path to the fire pit, which I built with my beloved partner, Ed, reminds me that the road of life isn't straight but rather has twists and turns, corners we cannot see around until we get there. Yet, we will arrive eventually.

My father's homemade wishing well, which I took from his yard upon his death, sits in the backyard as well, reminding me to keep dreaming, keep wishing, and keep setting goals to reach those dreams. There's no limit to what we can do with focus, determination, and inspiration!

The playhouse reminds me to keep delighting in life, as a child does, to remember to have fun, laugh, and not take myself too seriously. The little angel statue reminds me to stay in touch with my spiritual side, to seek guidance in silence, and to trust in a plan greater than what I may know or understand. To believe in something bigger than myself and count on it, *always*, as I do my breath.

And the trees—the many, many trees surrounding me—tell me I can grow in the harshest of conditions and stand strong anyway. With a solid root system, no storm can take me down. Just as I offer various kinds of food to the birds, we offer ourselves up to the world around us. Some will receive what we have to offer gladly. Others will not. People, experiences, and opportunities will come and go, just like the birds and the seasons throughout the year.

Through it all, I stayed steady with everything I know to be true, which I have shared with you in this book. And that brings us back to you. You picked up this book because something inside you said it was time for a change. You knew instinctively mid-life did not have to be the season of turmoil or tragedy it appeared to be. You wanted to look forward to the rest of your life, not dread it. As you've awakened, you've seen how you've made choices all along that led to the crossroads you're experiencing now. You've learned you have control over yourself and your life, so your mid-life makeover is up to you! You've gotten much clearer about how you want your life to look in every area. You've realized the necessity of letting go of things, beliefs, relationships, old habits, and old stories that have been a part of your life for a really long time. You've begun to clean up your messes and incompletes with a strong vision for how you want your environment to look and feel from now on. You've made your mind your best friend. You've begun to practice new habits and new daily routines that will support you in experiencing greater joy and meaning. You've stepped into leadership in your own life by taking care of yourself first and foremost, living life on your terms, and sustaining a life you can feel really good living. You realize now how beneficial all of this is to everyone around you and the impact you can have by keeping up everything you've learned. You know for sure your life isn't over; you just gave yourself a makeover!

Your Makeover Continues

At the same time, this can all be a bit overwhelming, and you may be uncomfortable with the "new you" you're creating. Making changes isn't easy for anyone, especially if you feel alone in the process. You may wish you had someone to bounce ideas off of or share your experiences with who truly understands you because they're going through the same process.

What the Geese Can Teach Us

You know how geese fly in the V formation all the time? They aren't artists. They instinctively know that flying in that pattern while flapping their wings together actually moves them along more quickly and with less energy. When the goose in the front gets tired, it drops to the back where it's most supported by the energy from the others. Then the nearest goose to the front takes over the lead until it, in turn, gets worn-out and needs a break. They get to wherever they're going by supporting one another, literally lifting one another up and helping to manage their needs along the way. A support group at its finest! Building a solid support system sometimes means engaging in new relationships because as you change, some of your current relationships start to get even more uncomfortable. There's nothing like a group of like-minded people to uplift you even more, cheer you on, and hold you accountable to your goals. Others won't let you fall, but if you do, they will also be the first to pick you up and carry you forward! They will have your back, just as the geese do!

My Flock of Geese

Throughout the years of my mid-life makeover, training with the Jack Canfield Company introduced me to hundreds of people from all over the world. They became my geese. When I was struggling with myself, trying to make changes, they helped me face my fears. When I needed to be uplifted, they answered the call with encouragement and love. When I wasn't seeing clearly, they helped show me the way.

I managed my mid-life makeover more efficiently and less dramatically because I had an amazing group of people riding along with me. I also had a team of professionals teaching me new ways of thinking, being, and doing. Learning new mindsets, skill sets, and success strategies with experts who had lived the concepts themselves made a tremendous difference in the changes I was able to make. The environment they created through their workshops, trainings, and mastermind meetings all set the stage for emotional safety and transformation.

When you have a group of solid support people journeying with you, anything becomes more tolerable. They help you to see yourself from another perspective and offer a safe place for you to explore and grow. They celebrate your best days and accept you on your worst. They understand because they're also on a growth path and running into their own version of fears, blocks, or unsuspected curveballs. Facilitation and leadership from trained professionals add another element of emotional safety, brilliance, and accountability.

To continue your mid-life makeover beyond the pages of this book, I'd like to personally invite you to join The Mid-Life Makeover Group. This is a group-coaching program for women in mid-life learning to love themselves fully and live on their terms. The experience includes a private Facebook Group, live weekly classes online, virtual group-coaching sessions, and lifetime access to my exclusive online course, The Mid-Life Makeover Method, all packaged together with me as the teacher, coach, and facilitator. Together, we are growing and changing, each woman on a unique path based on her own definition of success and happiness.

Like Sonya, who came to the group unhappy with her body. She knew she needed to take better care of it but found herself neglecting it for so many years while caring for others. Sound familiar? With the support of The Mid-Life Makeover Group Sonya was able to find the courage to eat differently, start a regular exercise regimen, and learn to live mindfully, which lowered her stress levels and increased her daily joy.

Or Robin, who came to the group feeling unfulfilled in her career. Robin was in a chaotic business environment within a large corporation. She had been there for decades and couldn't see herself doing anything else. Yet, she was more than stressed-out, terribly burned-out, and highly anxious in her role. She wanted the flexibility of her own business and to be more creative in the process. Her relationships were being challenged by her overworking and intense dissatisfaction. In The Mid-Life Makeover Group, she was able to identify her top passions and learn how to incorporate them into her professional life. She found the courage to leave corporate America and start her artistic venture. She calmed down. Now, she not only enjoys her professional life more, but her personal relationships have also improved.

And then there's Colleen, who reinvented her relationships with her family and friends using the teachings of The Mid-Life Makeover Group. She learned new ways to communicate effectively and how to put up healthy boundaries in her life. She learned to recognize when a relationship was toxic and needed to end. She learned how to resolve conflict within the relationships that were very important to her to keep. She made new friends who have enriched her life as well. Colleen's self-esteem and confidence have risen dramatically from the awareness she gained and the changes she made. She attributes much of her success to the coaching and the support of the other participants.

As these women prove, along with so many others not mentioned, going through any kind of change can be easier and more fun with a group of people. A group of like-minded people on a journey together will uplift you even more, provide perspective when needed, push you to keep going when you feel like giving up, and never let you fall. You can join us here: *www.cindydwhitmer.com/mlmgroup*.

So Can You!

Congratulations on picking up this book, reading it, and beginning your mid-life makeover! I hope you already see how incorporating the ideas and steps shared will lead you to loving yourself fully and living on your terms, making mid-life the best years of your life so far!

As you continue down the path of greater joy, success, and happiness on your terms, take notice of how your personal changes uplift others. Notice the ripple effect of your growth, for as you operate through life more effectively and focus on what ignites and excites you, that energy will spark in others. People around you will feel better about themselves and be inspired to turn that positivity into action, which makes the world better for everyone. The more of us who become healthy, happy, contributing people, the wider the circle becomes of those who can truly make a profoundly positive difference on others.

If I can do it, so can you! Remember, I wasn't born with a secret formula to having a great life. I didn't draw a lucky card that no one else has access to. I learned my way and worked my way through all the pieces of my life, just as every woman you've met in this book did. *So can you!* No matter where you've been, what you've done, or what you've gone through up to this point, you can begin again today! So embrace the possibilities, and start your makeover from the inside out! I support you and applaud you for your courage, and I can hardly wait to see what happens next. The end of this book is just your beginning.

Bibliography

Brown, Brené. *The Gifts of Imperfection: Let Go of Who You Think You're Supposed to Be and Embrace Who You Are.* Center City, MN: Hazelden Publishing, 2010.

Canfield, Jack. *The Success Principles™: How to Get from Where You Are to Where You Want to Be.* New York: Harper Collins, 2007.

Coach U Inc. *Coach U's Essential Coaching Tools: Your Complete Practice Resource.* Hoboken: John Wiley & Sons, 2005.

Dyer, Wayne W. *Change Your Thoughts, Change Your Life: Living the Wisdom of the Tao.* London: Hay House, 2007.

Harris, Alexander. "U.S. Self-Storage Industry Statistics." SpareFoot. January 27, 2021. *https://www.sparefoot.com/self-storage/news/1432-self-storage-industry-statistics/.*

Hassan, Sarmad. "Top 15 Leadership Qualities That Make Good Leaders (2022)." Taskque. January 5, 2022. *https://blog.taskque.com/characteristics-good-leaders/.*

Hendricks, Gay. *The Big Leap: Conquer Your Hidden Fear and Take Life to the Next Level.* New York: Harper One, 2009.

Lexico. "Fear." Accessed April 23, 2022. *https://www.lexico.com/en/definition/fear.*

Murphy, Mark. "Neuroscience Explains Why Your Need to Write Down Your Goals if You Actually Want to Achieve Them." Forbes. April 15, 2018. *https://www.forbes.com/sites/markmurphy/2018/04/15/neuroscience-explains-why-you-need-to-write-down-your-goals-if-you-actually-want-to-achieve-them/?sh=499b3cda7905.*

Walesh, Stuart G. "Using the Power of Habits to Work Smarter." Helping You Engineer Your Future. Accessed April 23, 2022. *http://www.helpingyouengineeryourfuture.com/habits-work-smarter.htm.*

Recommended Resources

Want a peek inside my bookshelf? Well, here it is! Over the years, these books and authors have literally transformed how I live my life both personally and professionally. Every day, I turn to at least one for inspiration, guidance, and information, which always enhances my experiences. If you're looking for further study, I highly recommend these books.

The Power of Intention by Wayne Dyer

You Can Heal Your Life by Louise Hay

The Success Principles™ by Jack Canfield

Daring Greatly by Brené Brown

Stand Up for Your Life by Cheryl Richardson

The Four Agreements by Don Miguel Ruiz

Think Like a Monk by Jay Shetty

Thank & Grow Rich by Pam Grout

Loving What Is by Byron Katie

Infinite Possibilities by Mike Dooley

The Big Leap by Gay Hendricks

Ask and It is Given by Esther and Jerry Hicks

Acknowledgments

WRITING THIS BOOK HAS BEEN A LABOR OF LOVE BACKED BY A STRONG SENSE OF MISsion. My life experiences, both personally and professionally, ignited a desire in me to use my voice to impact as many people as possible by sharing what I've learned firsthand about how to live fully. Throughout my journey, I have felt a divine presence and power in my life. I am blessed beyond measure. Thank you so much for choosing to read this book.

Thank you to my book coach, Ashley Mansour, for teaching me how to write a solid book in a short period of time. Your encouragement, guidance, humor, and wisdom made the process a truly delightful learning experience I will always remember.

Thank you to Taryn Wieland, Kat Pederson, Chelsea Mongird, Olivia Robinson, and my entire editing and publishing team for all your creativity, expertise, support, and guidance while transforming the content into a finished, beautiful product. And thank you to Jojo at Johanna Dye Photography for the lovely author photo.

Thank you to Kevin Wessels, my business strategist, who helped me define my brand, identify my niche, and clarify my message, as well as for introducing me to Ashley.

Thank you to Darleen Schillaci—the peace of mind I have with you navigating my business alongside me is invaluable. For this particular project, I thank you for creating the perfect logo at crunch time. Thank you for *all* you do!

Thank you to all the women (past and present) who have given me the great privilege of being their coach or therapist. I wish I could list all of you by name, but my professional ethics (and my heart) require I protect your privacy. Each of you means far more to me than you may realize. I am truly inspired by your courage, your willingness to be vulnerable, your desire to grow, and your determination to live fully for the rest of your lives. Your willingness to do the work gives me the opportunity to fulfill my mission, and I hope the time we have spent together will forever impact your life even more than it has mine. Several of you have been secret contributors to this book as well by letting me anonymously share portions of your stories, and for that, I am equally grateful.

Many thanks to Jack Canfield, his team, and my fellow trainees who all entered my world when I was most desperate for a new way to live. My mid-life makeover started when I began learning what you teach. Paired with the loving, supportive atmosphere you, your team, and other students created, I could safely begin exploring who I really was and what I wanted my life to be and start the long journey of transformation. An extra special thanks to Michelle Kaplan and Tresa Leftenant for your ongoing friendship, valuable feedback, consistent presence, and camaraderie all these years later.

Thank you to the members of the Real Spiritual Entrepreneurs Network, who are constantly cheering me on, offering ideas, and keeping me in touch with the highest part of myself so I continue to live and work from a place of inspiration. Your wisdom, presence, and friendship truly mean so much to me. Pam Grout and Jay Pryor, thank you for your extra doses of time, attention, friendship, and professional support.

Many thanks to my friends who have been on the journey with me the longest and have provided exceptional support during the most trying times of my mid-life makeover: Jill Myers, Brooke Vandenbrink-Ross, Debbie Galbraith, Michelle Kaplan, and Tresa Leftenant.

Thank you to my children, Laura and Justin, for riding the rollercoaster of my mid-life makeover with me. I am particularly grateful for how well you navigated your parents' divorce and the fallout of that decision. No matter what twists and turns life continues to bring, I will always love you both and be grateful to be your mom.

And to my bonus family members: Danielle, Grace, Yomiran, Matt, Jojo, and Alaska. Thank you so much for letting me be a part of your lives and for the memories we've made so far. What a wonderful addition to my life you are! I love you all and look forward to many more years together.

Finally, I must thank my beloved, Ed, for your constant support and belief in me and the work I do. Your love is the sweetest blessing in this season of my life, and I am so honored to get to love you and share life with you every day. (*And yes, I will marry you.*)

About the Author

CINDY D. WHITMER HAS BEEN COUNSELING, COACHING, SPEAKING, AND WRITING for over thirty years, helping people create meaningful lives personally and professionally. In her midforties, she found herself at a crossroads—unhappy, unsatisfied, and unsure of what to do. Believing she could thrive in mid-life and beyond, she dove deep into learning how best to overcome her biggest struggles, began to truly love herself, and transformed the darkest parts of her life into a peaceful, joy-filled adventure. She currently lives in Lawrence, Kansas. Besides running her own business, she loves walking the trails around her home, communing with nature, traveling the world, petting her cat, playing games, putting together jigsaw puzzles, and passionately loving everyone in her midst. Believing the best is yet to come for anyone willing to do the work, she is on a mission to teach women everywhere how to love themselves fully and live on their terms.

To contact Cindy regarding speaking engagements, please go to *cindydwhitmer.com/speaking* and fill out the speaker request form.

To learn more about her private, group, and corporate coaching programs, visit *cindydwhitmer.com/coaching*.

For all media inquiries or other questions, please go to *cindydwhitmer.com/contactme*.

Made in the USA
Middletown, DE
03 June 2022

66581096R00080